JOURNEY
OF A
GRATEFUL LOTUS
by
Nanci Reason

Nanci Reason

ISBN-10: 10-061574771X
ISBN-13: 978-0615747712

For information on our workshops

Go to :

www.unlimitedmiracleproductions.com

DISCLAIMER

The people and events have been changed to protect the innocent, and any similarities to actual persons, either living or dead, are merely coincidental.

Nanci Reason

Acknowledgements

First of all, I would like to thank all of you who played a major role in helping me "Make it Through", you know who you are.

I would like to thank my parents, Walt and Helen Niles, for joining my life with Nature and never instilling a sense of fear.

I would like to thank my German grandmother, Catherine Mechnig Niles, for giving me her strength and heritage.

I would like to thank my dear sister Carole Niles Casano who has always supported me and held my hand.

I would like to thank my wonderful son, Jason, for turning out to be such a wise and kind man, who has loved me unconditionally.

I would like to thank Carolyn for being such a wonderful Christian babysitter for Jason the first seven years of his life and for being an example to me of a Godly wife, mother and friend. In spite of taking so much flack over the years from the other parents that she was "enabling" me, she continued to have unwavering faith that one day I would become a Christian. I know, without a doubt, that if it were not for her continual prayers for me all those years, I would not have made it through.

I would like to thank all the failed relationships as they have mirrored back to me, my flaws, doubts and strengths so that I could experience a true transformation.

I would like to thank the Reverend Kyra Baeur for being my bridge so I could cross over from the box of religion to find my true self in spirituality.

I wish to thank the cancer for taking me to a higher spiritual level where miracles occur.

I would like to thank the long, dark nights when I was led by my angels and spirit guides. At their insistence they have written at least half of this book, which I couldn't have done without them. Thanks for continually waking me up.

I would like to thank my good friend, Janet, a raw food chef who helped me through the chemo treatments with deliveries of healthy foods. Without her love and support, I don't know if I would have made it.

I would like to thank my good friend, Patty, for helping me for the past year and a half by editing this work. If it weren't for her, these papers would still be sitting in a shoe box.

Last, but not least, I thank you, my readers. I have felt your presence on every page. Thank you for being willing to take this journey with me.

JOURNEY OF A GRATEFUL LOTUS

By

Nanci Reason, L.O.T.U.S.[1]

PREFACE

Once upon a time in another land lived a woman who, after twenty years of drug use and the lifestyle that went with it, became a born-again Christian. While on this new path into a new world and for the next eight years, because of the chronic psychological, physical and emotional damage, she frequently had to check into local crisis mental health and rehabilitation facilities. During a stay in one of those facilities, a fellow patient asked her, "Did you ever hear of anyone making it through all of this?" Her reply was, "No, I never have. But if I do, I will come back and tell them of my journey."

There have been many famous and infamous people that didn't make it through. She did. This is her story. So, come along with her on this journey of truth and transformation. You will be guided by a Cloud of Love by day and a Pillar of Passionate Fire by night.

****

---

[1] L.O.T.U.S.: Loving Others Through Unconditional Service

Okay, truth be told, I have been aware of Spirit's promptings that I should write this book for a long time. Until now I have not wanted to "go back". After all, it took years of drugs, booze, multiple suicide attempts, counseling, hopelessness and a river of tears to get through my "Trek in the Desert".

Why would I want to remember? Why would I want to feel everything all over again? Why would I want to forsake everything near and dear to me, to have the strength, resources and time to write it all down?

"Why?" you ask. Because I now realize that I can lay myself down as a bridge for you to cross over into the "Promised Land". If you are reading this please know that you are loved and you are worthy. This book will teach you that your first thought should always be one of truth. I thank you and honor you for taking this journey with me. When you set out to help yourself, you will wind up helping others.

CHAPTER 1

I was the second daughter born to Walt and Helen Niles. They named me Nanci. My birth was so lovingly awaited that Walt and Helen felt little concern that the Boston nor'easter was building mountainous snow drifts outside the military hospital. My birthing happened in the dead of winter as I joined the family of a career member of the US Army Air Corp (later to become the US Air Force). Needless to say this meant a transitory young life. Would you believe two tours to the Alaskan tundra, followed by posts spent in the warmer climates of Texas, New Mexico, California and Florida – a great opportunity to thaw out. The Air Corps stationed Dad at Elmendorf Air Force base in Anchorage, Alaska, for two adventure-packed years. Mother, with her refined Bostonian upbringing and determination to remain with her husband, swallowed hard and grabbed at her composure while landing there in 1947. The desolate grey tin Quonset huts scattered among the snow drifts gave her an instant picture of military life on the frontier. Talk about a culture shock! With our base housing not yet ready, they assigned us to live in one of these huts, equivalent to a tarpaper shack. No fine department stores for shopping, just the base personnel exchange. Not much pavement, just muddy ruts called roads. Friends and family lived far away and our neighbors included only a few Eskimos. This was going to be a unique adventure!

I must pause to tell you about my dad. He was a very high-spirited, adventuresome, determined guy. He loved to fish, fly airplanes and hunt. He was passionate about the great outdoors. Mmmmm! I wonder if dad actually volunteered for this assignment?! Dad gifted me with a sense of wonder and a love for exploring the outdoors. Apparently I had a much more adventurous spirit than my sister because a snapshot reveals a two-year old (me) tied to the dog house along with our husky, Smoky. Obviously this was to abruptly and finally stop me from any long investigative walks onto the frozen tundra as I headed for the magnificent Mount McKinley.

I'm sure that dad was also responsible for my exhilarating rides in those speeding dog sled races during the fur rendezvous. Oh, the fur rendezvous! Each spring the trappers would come to town from parts unknown, bringing furs and hides to be sold or traded to the Eskimos. At the same time the Eskimos held their own celebrations, thanking their gods for another good season. It was a wonderful, colorful and exciting time. Eskimo royalty mingled throughout the crowds wearing beautiful parkas embroidered with bright, bold colors; beautiful, smiling brown faces were framed by fur trimmed hoods. The smoke of huge bonfires filled the air. Fur trappers played festive music on their harmonicas and small accordions. Yes, indeed, I have vivid recollections of going to the fur rendezvous. In one especially joyful memory, a trapper's strong hands are tucking me down in his dog sled between blankets and cargo. I hear him yell, "Mush," and we are propelled over the snow for my first ever dog sled race. What fun!

Another fascinating memory was a trip to an Eskimo cemetery. I discovered that each grave had, standing over it, an ornately carved, brightly painted "house" about a foot and a half tall, that was put there by loved ones to house the spirit of the dead. Ironically, each building had a cross on top of it symbolizing an acceptance of Christianity. The totem poles and colorful miniature neighborhoods left a lasting impression. More than that, I developed a love for these dear Eskimo people who didn't even have a word in their vocabulary for "land measure" because of the vastness of their world. These earliest years developed and shaped long-lasting feelings and attitudes. Living in this unique environment where I was surrounded by the majestic Alaskan wilderness planted a deep appreciation for Nature in my soul, and by moving from one duty station to another I happily surrendered to an innate wanderlust. My first Alaskan adventure was coming to an end.

CHAPTER 2

Soon it was time to trade the boots and parkas for jeans and cowgirl boots as we followed our car's hood ornament down the highway. The world was transformed into long rows of telephone wires, blue skies, panoramic views, rust-colored plateaus and purple mountains. Yes, you guessed it – Texas! Yeehaw! This was going to be fun, I thought, as I roamed around the abandoned farm that my family had stopped to explore on the way to our new housing in Victoria, Texas. I mean, why go directly to our assigned destination when there were so many new places to feel, smell and see.

Living in a wilderness environment had a positive effect on our family. We had grown close and had chosen to do most things together. For example, Sister's hand (let me interject here that my sister's name is really Carol, but I always refered to her as "Sister"); anyway, her hand always stretched out to hold onto mine whether we were walking to school or crossing a stream. Dad was very protective and seemed always available -- either as a partner for a Ferris Wheel ride at the carnival or as a savior coming to my rescue when he heard me yell, "Daddy, help" (probably waist-high in stinging grasses). Our family was small -- Mom, Dad, Sister and I --

but full of fun! For instance: sing-ins, bingo at the base pool (where I put a jumping frog down the back of mother's dress one night), swimming, camping, and sewing strings of popcorn with Mom for the Christmas tree. The message loud and clear was: enjoy life to its fullest.

Dad developed a close friendship with a nearby rancher, Hank. When Dad purchased a palomino horse named Frisco we stabled him with Hank. That meant many frequent visits so we could ride and we learned a bundle about ranch life. We watched the ranch hands soak their new ropes in salt-water brine and bake them in a hot oven in order to transform them into lariats for rodeo events. This was my first impression of what a oven was for, not biscuits. While out on the range one day I huddled in the backseat of an abandoned car with Hank's youngest son while a huge Brahma bull kept charging and ramming the car. We yelled for help and finally our dads came to the rescue.

Along with the smells and sweaty excitement of calf-roping practices and rodeos, there was another fun, regularly scheduled event -- the original "Saturday Night Live" stock car races. These were held on the property directly adjacent to the ranch. As a result, we had a first-rate seating area located on the flat-top roof of the nearby "tack" house. We nailed down some chairs on the homemade viewing stands. Mother declined to climb the ladder and chose to observe the races from ground level. Dad, Sister and I climbed right up to view "topside".

The fun-filled days of singing "Camp Town

Races" and eating giant hamburgers were interrupted briefly by a flight to Tampa, Florida and a visit with my maternal grandparents. Grandmother was okay, but she was not very loving. Grandfather was great! A real adventurous outdoors man, Grandpa probably initiated their relocation from Boston due to his asthma. He also had a desire to develop a sailboat building enterprise which resulted in a lot of time spent on the ocean. I remember while out sailing my sister and I watched colorful sunsets and Grandpa always seemed to be climbing the center mast to adjust some rigging. Many days were also spent on the beach holding on to Sister's hand while exploring waves and sea shells on deserted beaches. Of course, posing and waving for pictures and playing ball with Daddy were all part of our day.

We also took a family trip to the city of Providence, Rhode Island, for a short stay with paternal grandparents. This couple was from the old country. If you could hear them talk, you would know in a minute they were German. "Vat do you vant to eat?" Grandma would lovingly ask in her German accent. She would prepare weinershnitzel, sauerkraut and delicious black bread for the family to enjoy and belch over later. She was a very large, strong woman who came to the United States as an indentured servant. Working for a wealthy family for one year paid for her passage. Grandpa was of slight stature and a big heart. He was good for taking us on walks to the park to feed the pigeons. When nap time came around, I was told to go lie down on the day bed in the dining room and watch for the cuckoo bird to come out of the clock. I was lulled to sleep by the tick-tock and

the soft voices of the adults savoring coffee and conversation.

This restful vacation and cordial time spent with family and loved ones was taken to prepare the family for more goodbyes and a second tour to the Alaskan tundra.

CHAPTER 3

This Alaskan tour was filled with more dog sled races, military air shows and the purchase of a maroon-colored Studebaker that needed a lot of pushing to get through the deep snow.

While traveling down forest-lined roads we stared in awe at the desolate Alaskan beauty on our way to camping and hunting expeditions. During the warm, summer days we enjoyed outside activities like doll carriage parades and games of marbles with the neighborly Eskimo children.

It was during this tour that mother began dealing with feelings of discouragement and frustration. Life was hard for a woman on the Alaskan frontier in those days. Even though we had hot and cold running water and electricity, there were environmental issues to deal with. For example, if a person decorated a home in the Southwestern United States, it might consist of Indian artifacts, wall hangings and clay pots. If decorating a home in the Midwest, it would be decked out with homemade quilts, crocks and farm items. However, in the wilds of Alaska, mother found herself dealing with the huge black bear rug (made from dad's largest kill) that sprawled with its face still growling and large, claw-laden paws outstretched across the middle of the living room floor. Because my sister and I thoroughly enjoyed snuggling into the warm, coarse fur, giggling joyfully as we used the bear's head for our own headrest, dad felt compensated for providing the bear rug. My mother, on the other hand, found it deplorable! Can you imagine having to lift the tail and head regularly to clean under? Not to mention the large expense incurred at the taxidermist. Mother often remarked that we could have taken a nice vacation for the family with that money.

When dad announced at the dinner table one evening that the family would be moving to Albuquerque, New Mexico, we girls excitedly asked him what it would be like; we were totally open to changing friends, schools, and teachers.

CHAPTER 4

Mother, meanwhile, quietly began packing the travel-worn cardboard boxes she had saved. The family traveled by car as the household goods were shipped ahead. Our leisurely trip included a stop in Northern California to see the magnificent giant redwood forests and to take more pictures (as if we didn't already have enough pictures of us smiling and waving in front of trees). Also along the way, we definitely had to stop in Arizona to experience the Grand Canyon, complete with mule rides. Our new home was located on a lovely tree-lined street in an "off-base" neighborhood. We easily made childhood friends; relationships close enough that we felt very lonely and sorrowful when a good friend couldn't come out to play for a few days because she had her tonsils removed. Other New Mexico memories include losing my front teeth while sitting on the back porch steps with a recuperated friend, eating a blueberry Popsicle and posing with a new boxer puppy for dad's homemade movies. Because we lived in a neighborhood of mostly "homeowners", rather than military travelers and nomadic Eskimos, we had a sense of being "established". Life in New Mexico was great but short-lived when dad, the zealous airman, announced that we needed to pack up and head for yet another tour – this time near Houston, Texas. It was far enough

away from our previous assignment in Texas
that we wouldn't be able to see old friends.
Goodbyes were becoming noticeably more
difficult as we grew older.

On the road again, we headed down the
country highway. It is strange how traveling can
breed a sense of familiarity, while at the same
time things are so very different. For instance, as
we settled in, we exchanged Alaskan mountain
lion hunts for a kitchen window view of jack
rabbit hides hung by the ears with mother's
clothespins on the backyard clothesline. I also
remember asking mother, "Can we keep it?" as
she discovered a live armadillo in the washing
machine. Our life this time was okay for the
family, but very different from our previous
Texas tour. No more ranch life with its horses,
lariats and stock car races. However, the family
soon fell into a "normal" routine of work, school
activities and a trip to the base pool for a
refreshing summertime swim. Everything was
recorded for all time in dad's movie camera.

Suddenly, Dad announced one evening that
our lives were about to change yet again. He had
scheduled an overseas tour of Europe. Of course
that entailed more packing, not to mention
passports, and shots. The next few weeks were
busy with getting inoculated. I assure you Sister
and I didn't like getting all those shots, but we
gritted our teeth through the ordeal knowing
we'd be rewarded with something special – a
concho belt or maybe a lovely doll. In addition,
excitement filled the air. We knew we would be
visiting second cousins that still lived in
Grandmother's village in the Black Forest in

Germany. What a great opportunity to learn about a different culture – its food, currency, language and lifestyle.

Days and weeks passed. We watched mother obediently sorting through outgrown clothing and unnecessary household items. We took trips to the base for dental appointments. We had no inkling of what was to come as mother loaded Sister and I into a car with only two packed suitcases.

CHAPTER 5

After what seemed like a fairly short trip
across America, Mother, Sister and I found
ourselves entering the state of Massachusetts.
Immediately, I sensed something was wrong;
everything got dark and quiet. My mother rented
an apartment near her mother in Quincy and
went to work in Boston. I was very rebellious
and upset with the whole situation. My
grandmother was always fussing at me over
what seemed like trivial things. There was no
explanation of why my dad was not there, only
silence. There was no love or nurturing for this
sensitive child. I remember hearing my
grandmother telling my mother, "I'll take Carol,
but I won't take Nanci." That put a hurt in me
that I carried around for 40 years.

Time passed and a new situation arose: my
mother brought a "friend" into our house. A man
named Salty. He was always doing something
with the ocean – clam digging, boating, etc., thus
the nickname. He was nothing like my debonair
father. Salty was one of Darby's original
"Rangers" – rugged, sloppy, and smelling like low
tide. He was my mother's high school
sweetheart, who later became the town drunk.
In my heart I thought, "Mother, have you
completely lost your mind?" Nothing was right.
Life as I knew it was gone. Family outings

consisted of going for rides to various beaches. We children played while the adults sat in the car and "talked". There was no family interaction.

Eventually Mom and Salty married in a secret wedding ceremony (my sister and I didn't attend). Salty was just there in our home one day. I became very upset. My school grades dropped due to a lack of concentration. I packed a bag and ran away to a local pond frequently. I wanted my life back. My sister, who was four years older, made friends and "adjusted". I felt utterly hopeless to the point that I began biting my friends. It was always in the same place, the shoulder. One night, while spending the night at a friend's, I remember we were settling down into a bed made for us in the living room. I remember feeling very comfortable and loved as we wiggled and snuggled. For the first time in a long time I felt safe. Warmth poured all over me. As I bit her, an overwhelming feeling came over me. A feeling of an infant teething intensely on an item in order to ease the pain that now had affected the whole body, anything to get relief. As my friend's mother responded to her scream, I became turtle-like, pulling everything into a shell for safety. I don't remember much after that. They called my mother and she arrived quickly. We both looked at the wound. I saw a full mouth of teeth marks imprinted and some broken skin. I was very sorry as I realized I would lose this lovely girl as a friend. The biting happened on other occasions, but this was the worst. To keep me busy, mother enrolled me in ballet lessons, then I joined the Girl Scouts, then

I took up roller skating. But I always became embroiled in a new set of problems.

My anxieties surfaced in the form of bed-wetting. I couldn't control myself. I did not want to wet the bed. As I slept, however, I would dream that I was on the toilet and would just "go". Sometimes I would even check myself in a dream, to make sure I was really on the toilet. Yes, I was, I thought. But as I began to go, the wet warm urine would wake me up. I guess to show support for me, my mother would completely strip my bed each night when that happened, and remake it fresh.

Still a third night time incident manifested. This time it was sounds. As I lay on my pillow to go to sleep, I would hear a crunching sound. As I listened more intently, holding my heart quiet, I could tell that it was footsteps rustling through fallen leaves in the woods. Each time I drifted off to sleep I would think to myself "tonight I'm going to find out who it is that's making all this noise". Soon I was able to immediately go into an intense mode of listening. I began to visualize and I saw who it was – well, their feet anyway. It was witches coming from the forest and they were after me! After that I could hardly sleep at night. I tossed and turned, afraid they would get me. I pushed this so deep inside of me as a way of coping, that I could not tell my mother what was wrong because consciously I couldn't remember. This went on for several years. Finally in my adult life, and this is unbelievable, I discovered it was my hair rubbing against my ear that made the sound that hounded me for years.

All of this, coupled with a loss of self-esteem, made my life unbearable. There were problems at school also. I was unable to function. I acted out all the time. I fidgeted, I couldn't sit still. My mother finally took me to a psychiatrist. Even though it is acceptable now, it was simply unheard of in those days unless you were stark raving mad. I only remember a couple of visits with a lady. She was nice; she gave me a bracelet. She probably told my mother that I would be alright and sent me on my way. I was not able to snap out of it.

CHAPTER 6

We moved to a small peninsula town south of Boston called "Houghs Neck". There was one way in and one way out. Everyone knew everyone else's business. Houghs Neck consisted of a couple of bars, a market, a drug store, two variety stores and a skating rink. By the time I was in the sixth grade I had made friends with some pretty rough girls. I wanted to be tough so that no one could hurt me anymore. My mother had two more girls with Salty. At 42, she was overwhelmed with the responsibility of having two babies so late in life. In those days, 42 was very old for having kids, but the four of them became a family. My sister got married and moved in with her husband's family. Consequently I pretty much grew into a vessel of hatred for both my mother and Salty. Salty definitely did not want me around "his" children. "Fine," I thought as I realized I was on my own.

As time went along, I couldn't stand being in the house any longer with this family. My step-father walked around the house with his pants down to the crack of his butt and his hand was always down inside the front of them. Mother seemed overwhelmed with guilt and fear. She would not let Salty discipline me; consequently I received no discipline and had no boundaries. I was smoking in my bedroom at home and walking the streets with my girlfriends as an escape, dressed all in black.

When I was in the seventh grade I moved in with a young married couple that I babysat for. They encouraged me and life was great. I was on the other side of the peninsula; my grades improved to high honors. My mother would cash my allotment checks from my father and give me money to live on. I was on my own; I was happy.

Well, almost happy. I started looking for love and acceptance. I found it with the rebellious ones in the neighborhood; the guys that had a real zest for life. One summer night when I was thirteen the high school football hero and his friend met me and my girlfriend on the street. They asked us if we wanted to go have a couple of beers with them. Next thing I knew we were partying in the cottage next to the sub shop. Somehow the football players had gotten use of the cottage from Bill who owned the sub shop, which was the local hangout along with the cottage. Well, one thing led to another and I really felt that this guy was in love with me. After all, he had his arm around me and gave me a cigar band for a ring. "Wow!" I thought, "My first ring. This must be love." The next thing I remember was being in a dark bedroom with him on top of me and inside of me. It was very uncomfortable, emotionally and physically. When I got home, I got rid of my bloody underwear and went to bed feeling very dirty and dejected. I found out the next day that there was an intercom system between the cottage and the sub shop and that the whole incident had

been broadcast live to everyone within hearing
distance.

CHAPTER 7

That was the turning point in my life. No one was going to hurt me anymore. I WAS IN CONTROL. I excelled in school and got lots of acceptance and recognition. I was a party girl, but on my terms. I was good looking, well- built and I knew it. I slept with guy after guy but only when I wanted and with whom I wanted. I knew my mother was hurt by my reputation and I was glad.

The summer of '62 found me on the beach checking out a new blond guy who was showing off by water skiing with a chair on a disc. Pretty good, I thought. Approaching him in my risqué, two-piece bathing suit, I asked him where he was from. "Up there", he said, pointing to a flower-covered cliff that held an enormous house. He said his father was a contractor and his brother was an architect, so his family bought the old house and redesigned it. Sven was 19 and was home on leave from the Air Force.

After a couple of hours I was water skiing with the best of them. He taught me a lot about balance on skis and about boating in general. I was impressed by his intelligence. As the afternoon was coming to a close, he offered me a tour of the magnificent beachfront house and I accepted. This unimpressionable kid was impressed. There was a colored waterfall in the main entryway and a 24 foot wide panoramic window with a view all the way to Boston. "Your own private beach," I thought. "That is acceptable." The tour continued-- turquoise carpeting, bright, tropical print couches, fine china and a "bad" hi-fi stereo system. Upstairs there were expensive bedroom furnishings. While he was showing me his room, he locked the door and started chasing me around the bed. I managed to get out of the room because I remembered the "cottage" incident. I hollered "call me" as I ran down to the beach to get my things.

The summer was spent water skiing and boating with Sven's family; lots of fun visiting nearby islands for picnics and beach parties. Sven went back to the Air Force. I did not sleep with him because I wanted to hold out and make him suffer because he wanted me so badly.

Chapter 8

School started and life returned to "normal" - - walking the streets and partying. Through all this time, one guy had stolen my heart; his name was Ned. He was so sweet and funny and a drunk. He used to sing to me the song "Brown Eyed Girl". We made love all over that peninsula, off and on for about three years.

Eventually Sven got out of the Air Force and came home to work at his father's general contracting business. Our relationship resumed and I told my mother who I was seeing. She said, "Oh, you shouldn't see him; he's got a reputation with the girls." Alright! Mother didn't like him; all the more reason to see him. I turned 17 that year and I guess Sven's mother felt it was time to take me under her wing. I was to learn how to take care of a house properly including how to turn a mattress, vacuum and so on. She also taught me to make a highball and to dress and entertain properly. She would take me shopping and buy me rich items, like a coat. This was a whirlwind affair; it was acceptable.

It was August of 1964 when I found out I was pregnant. I didn't know if Sven or Ned was the father. I was seventeen and did not want to get married. When I told Mary Ann, the woman that I babysat for, she said, "I will help you. Do you have any money?"

"Yes, a little, I replied."

"Good. Let's go buy you an outfit and I'll take you where you can make some real money so you can get your own apartment – for you and the baby."

She picked out a very sophisticated baby blue Italian knit skirt suit with brown suede heels and pearl jewelry.

While she was fixing me up I felt like a Barbie doll; it wasn't me – just a "look". She drove us over to Logan Airport in Boston. We went to the cocktail lounge and Mary Ann checked in with the bartender. I was told to go to a certain room, get undressed, and wait there. The gentlemen stopped in one after another. Each one demanded something different for me to do. They were older, professional travelers like doctors and lawyers. Some were nicer than others.

On the way home I felt really, really low in my spirit. Although the money was good, I never wanted to do this again – have sex with so many strange old men. You see, when you are a prostitute you think that you are getting something back for something you are giving. But how can you put a price on your soul? If you are not standing in your truth about a certain situation, then you are prostituting yourself. I eventually realized years later that Mary Ann didn't want to help me; she wanted to help herself become a Madam. Those things happen when you don't "stand in your truth".

I went home, took a bath, called Sven and asked him to come over. As we sat on the front porch I began to cry as I told him that I was pregnant. He held me in his arms and said," It's okay, we'll get married." We drove over to his parents' house and told them. They were very accepting and encouraging. His father started making highballs for everyone. It was almost like a celebration. I definitely felt better. The next day I went alone to my mother's house and told her the news that I was pregnant and Sven and I were getting married. The wedding plans were on.

CHAPTER 9

It was a beautiful candle-lit ceremony. I wore
my sister's wedding gown and she was my
matron-of-honor. My father, who was back in
the states, came to give me away. As we
proceeded down the aisle I could not stop crying
and did not want to let go of his arm. I was no
longer in control.

Six months later my daughter, Cheryl, was
born. She was wonderful; the marriage was not.
Sven wanted sex all the time and I did not want
to submit on his terms. Anger began to fester
within us. He would go out in the boat night-
fishing and drinking with friends and come back
very hostile. We were renting a small house
located right between both parents' houses. I
was trying to be a "60's" wife and mother, it was
not fun.

Our first child was about to turn four
months old in September of 1963 and it was
time for me to get a part-time job for some
Christmas money. Housewives and mothers
didn't get out much socially in those days and,
being only 18, I was looking forward to working
outside the home and meeting new people. I
applied and was hired at the new discount
department store. It was big – something like K-
Mart.

I worked in a backroom called a "Marking
Room" running a machine that installed price

tags on the products. The store manager was a handsome single guy named Paul Hirsh. He was constantly asking me out and I kept replying "I'm married". Time passed and I found myself being transferred from one department to another. (This is why sex discrimination laws are so important today.) Paul told me that the transfers would continue and get worse until I went out with him. I never told Sven about this. I just went to work each evening. Eventually I found myself outside in the garden center marking lawn mowers in the cold! They were leftovers and Paul wanted sale tickets put on them. "Okay," I thought to myself, "this is getting ridiculous. I'm going to have to go out with this guy." So I made a plan. The annual employee's Christmas party was coming up and that would be the perfect time. I put on a sexy black chiffon dress, heels, did my hair and went to the party. After drinks and dancing, Paul and I slipped out to his place. Even though there were more drinks and sex, I managed to make it home quietly and slipped into bed unnoticed. I was laid off shortly after that. Even having sex with the boss doesn't ensure job security!

At 18, another pregnancy, and a year and 2 weeks after the first baby, another daughter was born. I did not want this child. She cried all the time, probably sensing what she was born into. I was up to my ears in diapers, formulas and fights with my husband. My only salvation during those turbulent years was my neighbor, Susan. She was the only young housewife and mother, beside myself, in the area. Susan also was in an unhappy marriage with three small children. We became best friends and spent each morning having coffee at her house while the children played. She was from California and would talk about it everyday. She used word pictures to describe the beautiful beaches, sunsets and the tall palm trees. Oh, how she yearned to go back there! To make matters worse, another good friend would come over and tell me about all the fun I was missing in my senior year at school. Ugh! I was so angry! My life was out of control, again. I did see my minister for counseling. All he did was fondle my breasts. I left there, frozen inside.

Three years of strife and fighting passed and one night my husband and I really got into it. He landed a blow to my jaw. That did it! I thought, "that is the last time he is going to touch me." I went to see an attorney the next morning and filed for a divorce.

CHAPTER 10

It was very difficult in those days for a single mother to make it on her own. I wasn't afraid. I moved myself and the kids into a sleazy rooming house. I went to work in the owner's office for a room and $60 a week. I made friends with some other girls that worked there and started partying again. In one of our favorite clubs I met a drummer I liked. One weekend he asked me to party with him at a gig in New Hampshire. I told my babysitter I'd be back at a certain time. Because I couldn't get a ride back, I didn't get home at the time I said I would and my babysitter called the police to report the girls "abandoned". The authorities called my in-laws and they took custody of my girls. I continued to work and waited impatiently for the divorce court date to arrive.

Since I had no car and my mother had no car and there were no buses to Dedham, on the morning of August 25, 1968 I got up, put on a nice dress and heels, teased my hair and walked to the highway near my house. With absolutely no fear I climbed over the road barrier and began to hitch a ride to the courthouse. It wasn't long before a trucker stopped and asked me where I was going. When I told him of my plight, that nice guy took me all the way to the front steps of the Dedham Superior Courthouse and I got there -- right on time! I often wondered if he were an angel.

We were all there: my in-laws with their corporate attorney who was also the court magistrate in the town we lived in (Quincy, Massachusetts), Sven, me and my $75 attorney. The case was called and the in-laws' attorney proceeded to read about my suicide attempt. This was an excerpt from a diary which I had written during my troubled teenage years. Sven had given them my diary to prove I was unstable and unfit to be a mother. I don't remember much after that. I'm sure my character was bombarded with more of their ammunition and my attorney offered little on my behalf. The divorce was decreed as I was sure it would be, but full custody of my two girls was granted to my in-laws. The court gave me visitation rights. I couldn't believe it! A bang of the gavel and it was over. The in-laws offered me a ride back to town and I took it. During the ride my mother-in-law offered to pay for me to go to beauty college. My reply was, "I don't want your money."

As they dropped me off at my apartment everything became very dark that day. It was another major loss since my father left. I was all alone. That day I believe that my soul (my mind, will and emotions) left my spirit and little Nanci just curled up in a ball somewhere and cried. I also believe that a piece of hopelessness jumped in my soul in the form of believing that nothing for me would ever last. This was something I would carry deep down inside of me for the next twenty years..

CHAPTER 11

My strong-willed spirit and my physical body continued to function. I must have moved because I remember living in an old rooming house but I don't know where it was or how I got there. Sven paid for it. Time passed and each day started and ended the same, with a deep feeling of loneliness and longing for my girls. Occasionally I would take some buses and go "visit" with my girls. I hated the fact that their grandmother would stand in the same room we were in, with hands on her hips and joyfully tell me all about the wonderful things she had bought them and done with them. She had always wanted girls and now she had mine. The pain was more than I could bear.

Everyday I would walk from my rented room to the corner market and buy a can of Spaghettios. That's all I ate for the day. Autumn came and went and winter arrived. I was still in the darkness and had gone down to skin and bones.

One cold winter day as I walked on the snow to the market, the sun came out and I saw the ice crystals. They were magnificent and they were on everything. I looked down at my feet and saw that I was walking on a path of sparkles; I looked up and they were hanging from tree branches – beautiful crystal icicles shimmering in the sunshine. The rows of houses looked like ice castles adorned with shining crystals. Oh, the sunshine on my face felt so good! I stood there with my eyes closed and took a deep breath of the clean, frosty air. When I opened my eyes, I said to "little Nanci", "It's going to be okay. We're not alone anymore because the ice crystals are here." Once again Mother Earth had revealed herself to me in all her radiant splendor – God's love. You see, only God gives us Nature; everything else is from man. That's the magic of Nature – reality versus illusion. I was able to respond with a little piece of myself and went out and got a job.

While working in the office one day I met a girl named Veronica. It was obvious that it would be financially advantageous for both of us if I moved in with her and her two kids. Also we both agreed that it would be a lot of fun.

CHAPTER 12

I was ready to have some fun. The first Saturday night after I moved in found us dressed up, looking sexy and excited to go out dancing. It was 1968. Mini-skirts and thigh-high boots were all the rage. I bleached my hair platinum and wore a waist long hairpiece with it. I wore contact lenses and plenty of makeup. I was young and hot and I knew it. Ronnie was a natural beauty from Madison, Wisconsin, with thick rich brown hair, green eyes and a beautiful smile.

We walked into the local dance club. That was the hot spot for partying because of its live bands. The bouncer checked out our IDs while we checked out the guys. We spotted a table with three good-looking guys sitting at it and decided to join them. The waitress came around and they ordered drinks for us. The good looking one to my right, Hal, asked me to dance. He was Irish and had played football for the Marine Corps. I liked the way he was built and the way he moved on the dance floor. He felt the same way about me. We drank, danced and laughed until the place closed. My roommate and I told the guys that we would meet them there next week and headed for home.

Tuesday came and we decided to shoot in a women's pool tournament that night in a small,

local bar called Sully's. It had really cold beer,
good looking barmaids and five great pool tables.
It was a hangout for all the top pool shooters in
the area. Loud Stones music on the jukebox
greeted us as we entered. I ran into an old friend
of mine from high school. His name was Robby
and I always had sort of a crush on him. He was
long and lean; the strong silent type and tonight,
available. Shot some pool and got eliminated
early. I didn't care because I wanted to focus on
Robbie. He asked me if I wanted to get out of
there and I told my roommate I would see her
back at the house.

Robbie had a van and we drove over to an
isolated area near the beach. We made love all
night long. It was great but then it was over. I
just wanted to sleep with him one time. The
belief that everything was temporary and would
never last had taken root deep in my soul.

CHAPTER 13

The following Saturday night we went back to McGuires and found the guys. They were glad to see these fun-loving party girls. Hal asked me if I wanted a "black beauty." "What's that?" I asked. "It's speed and you can stay up all night long," was the response. "Sure," I said as I swallowed it down with a drink. Whew! I felt great! We danced all night. We closed the place again and Hal and Joe came home with Ronnie and me.

What happened next was the ride of a lifetime. Non-stop sex all night long! We even broke the bed, put a suitcase underneath it and kept on going! I was in love, lust or something with this guy.

The next day we went out for brunch and he took me over to the local bar where he hung out. It was over in Quincy, called O'Malley's Pub. It looked like Christmas in there. All kinds of things lay all along the bar -- men's cashmere coats, watches, rings, radios, women's exquisite suits and purses; even large pieces of meat. He explained to me that the "fences" were here and they would buy your shop-lifted items for 50% of their value. They would pay you $100 for a $200 man's cashmere coat. Not a bad day's wages in 1968. He asked me if I wanted to team up with him and be his "blocker". A blocker was someone that would stand between any employees and the empty shopping bag he would carry. It was so easy. This was before the days of security cameras.

We became a great team. We traveled all over the south shore area. We only had to "boost" (shoplift) two to three $200 coats a week to make plenty of money. The rest of the time was spent partying and screwing. I had a fantastic wardrobe of sexy dresses and high-class suits.

During this time I found myself pregnant again. I didn't care if it was Robbie's or Hal's. I wasn't going to have another child to lose again. I told Hal that I wanted to make arrangements with a friend of his who was a professional abortionist. Because it was illegal in those days, the service cost $100. But because they were friends, he did mine for free. "Wow," I thought, what a good friend to do the coat hanger and green liquid procedure on a dirt floor basement for free!"

Hal and I continued with our shoplifting for about a year. The only problem was that Hal was married to a woman who lived on the north shore of Boston. Any holiday or kid's birthday and he was gone for a while. Boy, that used to piss me off! Christmas was coming and I decided that if Hal didn't spend it with me, I would go to California since there was nothing left here for me. He didn't, so I called my girlfriend, Susan and asked her if she still wanted to go to California. She said "sure!" We set a date for January 22, 1969.

Journey of a Grateful Lotus

CHAPTER 14

It was February 22, 1969, the day after Joe Namath and the New York Jets won the Super Bowl. My girlfriend, her three kids and I packed a few worldly possessions into my 1957 Ford station wagon and headed for San Diego where her father lived. It was the year of Woodstock, peace signs, Janis Joplin and Jimmy Hendrix. Anyone over 30 was not to be trusted. Vietnam. Martin Luther King and the Kennedys. Civil rights marches held by people that just wanted a little respect. Hippies, marijuana, free love, communes, flower power. The Beatles' life-changing music. LSD and a chance to expand the mind. The "generation gap" was formed and a chasm between generations created. Tie-dyed t-shirts. Organic was everything. "Sex, drugs, rock and roll" was coined. The air was electric. Draft dodgers went to Canada, others went to Woodstock-- the concert of the century. There is nothing to compare it with, either before or since. There was a spirit of hope in the youth of America; we knew we could change the world. To what, no one knew, but we were going to have one heck of a time finding out.

This was our world as we set out in a car covered with stick-on flowers and a rear window sign that read, "California or Bust". All I needed to get there was sheer determination, plus a hot credit card from a friend, some Benzedrine to stay awake, and a picture of my boyfriend taped on the dashboard to remind me why I was leaving. After seven days on the highway eating mostly bologna sandwiches, we arrived at our destination. It was beautiful in California, but most of all it was warm! I was finally in the land of opportunity; here was my chance for a fresh start!

I always had a knack for hairdressing, so that was what I planned to pursue. My girlfriend and I got a cheap apartment on the south side of San Diego in Chula Vista. I got a job as a waitress in an Italian restaurant and ditched the car so it couldn't be traced from the hot credit card I used for gas. In need of another car, I put on a very low-cut sundress, heels, did my hair and proceeded to go car-hunting. I found a small car dealership; the middle aged owner was checking me out through the window. Thinking this was a likely spot to find a used car, I entered the lot and bent over to inspect a red corvette convertible as he approached me. Showing my cleavage to its best advantage, I mentally said to him, "Come on honey, come a little closer." I told the guy I needed a car, and that I was willing to do "anything" for it. After a couple of dates I was driving a Plymouth fury.

Life was good. I enjoyed my job and was saving up money for uniforms and shoes for beauty college (the only things not financed by a Government grant for tuition that would be paid back at a later date). Naturally I wanted to earn as many tips as possible, so I shortened all my waitress uniforms to a tight "thigh-high" miniskirt length. I was also making friends. We would close the restaurant at 1:00 a.m. Sunday mornings, take some Benzedrine or speed and head for the all-night discos of Tijuana. I had a goal and was working towards it. I wasn't sleeping with anyone and in general I felt good about myself. On the other hand, my roommate wasn't doing too well. I didn't realize it at the time, but she was getting hooked on the hard stuff. I sensed that she was "main-lining" heroin but there was no real evidence of it around the house. "Oh well," I thought, "To each his own. It'll be okay."

At work I got a daily dose of self-esteem from a good-looking middle aged Argentinean customer who owned the appliance shop next door to the restaurant. He lived in an apartment in the back of his appliance store. He was always trying to go out with me. "Yuk," I thought, "I don't want to go out with this dirty old man, not just for fun anyway." How close I got to letting him grab my butt depended on how big a tip I wanted that day. I was a good waitress. I knew how to "work the customers". I WAS IN CONTROL and loved it!

CHAPTER 15

Weeks passed. Then one day a broken-hearted kid, the dishwasher at the restaurant, lost his girlfriend because she had moved with her parents to Reno, Nevada. When he asked me to drive him up there to see her, I said, "Sure, no problem" and we headed out the following Friday night after work. When we were way up in the mountains, the car engine decided to blow up. I asked this kid where we were going to stay. "With some friends of mine," he replied and that was good enough for me. So we abandoned the car on the side of the road and hitchhiked into town. We were picked up by a Volkswagen with four airmen in it. Somehow we crawled onto laps and made it to town. It was two or three in the morning as we walked through the main street of town. The only signs of life were a couple of drunk Indians huddled in a store-front. A strange feeling came over me that something wasn't quite right. It was the same feeling that I'd had when I entered Massachusetts as a kid. I just shrugged it off.

We approached the home of his friends where we were going to stay, I was surprised to see all the lights on. Come to find out this was the home of seven airmen that were stationed at the base nearby. All of them had taken some LSD and one was sitting up in a tree in front of the house. "Hello," he said cheerfully as he sat

perched on a limb eating a bowl of Jell-O. Right
away I knew this was going to be a very
interesting visit. As we entered the house it was
obvious that several other people were high on
acid doing various things, like staring at a wall
or cooking strange things and laughing
uncontrollably. At that point I realized that I
could not stay there and somehow had to get
back to San Diego. It was my first real feeling of
"every man for himself".

I tried to call my roommate, Susan, with no
success; no one was home. Then I thought of the
Argentinean. He would wire me $100 for a bus
ticket. So I called him and he sent the money.
Because he was busy when my bus arrived in
San Diego, he sent his partner to pick me up.
Joe was good looking, had a "bad" T-Bird and a
jealous wife. When we pulled up to my
apartment something didn't look right, so I told
Joe to wait while I checked it out. The doors
were locked and bolted so I looked through the
windows. The place was completely empty – bare
floors, bare walls. Susan was gone, along with
all my worldly possessions. I was in the streets
with nothing but the clothes on my back. I told
Joe to take me to the Argentineans'. "Great," I
thought, "now I'm going to have to sleep with
this guy till I get on my feet."

Everything from that point on is fuzzy. The
Argentinean kept me high on something and for
several weeks I was locked up in the rear of his
apartment and used for various sex acts. While I
was there, I could not think clearly or put up a
fight; I was totally stoned, 24/7. I don't even
know if he fed me the drugs directly or if he put

it in my food. I had no one to turn to for help. Eventually the "fog" lifted a little. I don't know if I had developed a tolerance or his stash was running out. But I knew I had to get out of there. Somewhere in the back of my mind I remembered that Joe had a jealous wife. I figured that if I let her know where I was, she would free me. I had to find her phone number. I vaguely remember searching the place for it when the men were gone. My plan worked, because when I called Joe's wife and told her of my predicament, she said she would be right over. The only way out of the place was to bust out the store-front window, so that is what we did. I was free! I recall taking a breath of fresh air as I jumped into her "getaway car". I told her that, for obvious reasons, she would have to take me somewhere where the men would never find me. She said she had the perfect place. I would stay with a friend of hers; a single mother with her own home on the other side of town. That sounded good to me.

CHAPTER 16

We drove for awhile and finally arrived at the place where I would stay. We walked inside and I met my new roommate, Diane. She was an attractive redhead, a bubbly and friendly bartender. Diane was divorced with three beautiful little girls. Although she had a boyfriend who helped her financially, she was trying to make it on her own.

Because I wanted to find work, I needed to rebuild my wardrobe. One day I said to Diane, "Come on, I'll get you some clothes for letting me stay here." We went to the nearby mall and I started lifting clothes right and left. "You just stand beside me and block me," I told her. We worked well together. After several trips to the car with goods, I was in a frenzy. The high I got from all of this was feeding on itself. I wanted more. We went into a high class department store, where I started lifting a ring, a watch and some other jewelry boldly out of a case. Needless to say, we got busted and taken to jail. Diane called her uncle who owned an adult bookstore downtown; he bailed us out. Since we were only arrested for the couple of items in that one department store, we cautiously walked to our car which was still full of stolen goods, and drove home. I was now in a position to go to work. As an experienced bartender in the area, Diane made good on her offer to get me a job tending bar. We worked the same shift so I could ride with her to work until I got a car. I was on the way up again. I sloughed off all the "come-ons" and advances made to me by the customers. Guess I didn't realize that the low-cut mini-dresses were part of the problem. To me, my sexy clothes were just the "uniform of the day". As for guys, "who needed them," I thought. I was on my way to Beauty College and nothing was going to stop me.

It was a quiet weeknight. I was tending bar with thoughts of closing up early. Only a couple of "regulars" stuck around; they would probably leave by 11:30. The night was dragging on. Diane called to say that her boyfriend had a buddy who was on his way over to check me out. It was also dead where Diane worked and they would be over to my place soon. I hung up and Harry walked in. Jeans, boots, denim jacket, blue knit stocking cap. He had a trimmed beard, copper-colored skin, green eyes, golden hair. He looked like a young Charlton Heston. He was electric. "Not too shabby," I thought. "This evening might turn out to be interesting after all." He introduced himself and ordered a beer. I continued to "pace myself" for an early closing – keeping the beer stocked, unused ashtrays washed, clean glasses put away. Harry sat at the middle of the bar where the sinks were located; this was where a bartender spent a lot of time. I asked him to "shake for the music" (a dice game played between the house and the customer, the loser feeding the jukebox). This served two purposes; the first because you could usually read a person by the songs he played and secondly, there's nothing worse than being in a bar when the music stops and reality sets in. I played the music and probably chose something cool in that time, like "I Am Woman" by Helen Reddy.

Harry asked me to shoot a game of pool. I checked on the couple of remaining customers and they were okay. I felt that coming out from behind the bar to shoot pool was telling the customers they weren't as important as my personal pleasure. In reality, this was probably true.

Pool is a great sport. Not only for accuracy, but also because it involves "body language" and psychology. Harry read my body language and I studied his physique. He was handsome. A well put together body with long arms and gorgeous hands. Besides what I could see, there was a quiet, still, inner strength about him; almost an aristocracy or royalty. He said he had some American Indian in him, so I decided that was probably where this quality came from.

Diane and her boyfriend arrived. I poured them a pitcher of beer. Laughter was in the air. Her boyfriend was a funny guy. I discovered that he had told Harry earlier in the evening at a pool tournament that he should check out the new roommate. "She's from Boston and talks real funny." We shot some pool and the regulars left. I began closing the bar. The guys helped by putting up the bar stools and we were soon out of there.

Since I was the only one without a vehicle, I jumped on the back of Harry's motorcycle – bare legged and wearing sandals. The neighborhood was a hilly one and we were playing follow the leader. At one point I thought Harry was going to crash into a parked truck. So - I stuck my right foot out in a reflex action and "Bam!" caught it on the truck's bumper and laid it open.

CHAPTER 17

When we got to our house, Diane got some bandages which she handed off to Harry. As he began doctoring my foot, Diane and her "better half" retired to the bedroom. Harry told me he had worked as a nurse. "Yeah, right", I thought. "He'll start at my foot and work his way up." I still had no desire to let a man close to me.

Harry got my foot bandaged and we sat at the kitchen table and talked until morning. He never made a pass at me. "Strange," I thought, "but nice." My foot was swollen and sore. Around 10:00 a.m. I called my boss to explain what happened; that I couldn't work that night. His response was, "You're fired!"

When I shared this with Harry, he asked me if I had seen the ocean yet. "No," I responded. I accepted his invitation for a ride to the beach. I can remember arriving there very clearly. I was so overwhelmed by the beauty of the ocean and the size of the surf that I jumped in – clothes and all! This was the funniest thing Harry had ever seen, so, putting his money and keys in his shoes, he jumped in too! It was wonderful! So clean – so pure – so invigorating! We spent that day walking the beach, well -- he walked and I hobbled. We did a lot of sharing. I watched him as he looked out over the water so methodically before he spoke. He had charisma; his golden hair was blowing in the breeze; his facial features were accented by his straight nose, high cheek bones and meticulously trimmed beard. But most of all, I loved those eyes. Under strong wonderful eyebrows they were so piercing, looking so hard to find the answer.

There were no games; just honesty. It felt different from previous relationships – not heavy, but light, airy, fresh. We went back to Diane's house and when she asked me, "How's it going?" I told her "great." I also whispered to her the fact that I hadn't slept with him yet and he was still around. That first night I stayed at his apartment at the beach. Harry got out a pair of pajamas and gave me the top. "You wear that," he said, "and I'll wear the bottoms." "How strange," I thought. Still he didn't touch me. Was this guy normal or what, I wondered.

Several days later we found ourselves looking for a place to rent together. When we found a cute house with a For Rent sign in the window, we gave the owners a down payment and moved in. We set up shop with nothing but a bed in the living room, two TV trays, a used television set and some pots and pans. Harry had arrived in San Diego only a short time before I did; neither one of us had any household belongings.

Harry was from Texas and he was determined to "make it" out here. He worked construction as a journeyman drywall finisher. One day he invited me to pack a lunch and come to work with him to keep him company. I said, "okay". No more fancy hair styles. My dream of going to beauty college drifted away like one of the sailboats in Mission Bay.

CHAPTER 18

The weather now was hot and dry. Harry's job consisted of running a drywall tool called a "bazooka" because of the way it was shaped. It was about three feet long and about four inches in diameter. It held several pounds of drywall mud (which was pumped into it) and a roll of drywall tape on a spindle. As he rolled it over the joints, the mud and tape came out together and just sort of laid on the joint. Because it had to be "wiped down" as soon as possible before it dried, he didn't have much of a chance to really explain to me what he was doing.

This was a whole new world for me to explore. As days passed, I found myself digging around in the back of the truck for a mud pan and a drywall knife that I could use and began practicing wiping the tape down. After about a month, when he saw that I was serious about learning the trade, he began taking some time with me teaching me the use of some of the other tools. The whole situation grew and developed very smoothly.

Over the next few months, any fat that I had been packing around melted off and I started developing some serious muscles. Life was great! I loved the work and enjoyed being with Harry. After working hard all day, I would go home and cook a good supper, pack the lunches for the next day, and even go to the Laundromat. Back up at 5:00 a.m. the next day. Harry had started calling me "Lucille" after B.B. King's guitar because I had so much soul. The alarm clock would go off and he would say "Lucille, get in there and rattle those pots and pans." I was able to accomplish all this with a little help from my friends – whites, bennys and prescription diet pills. I eventually met some of his friends who dealt in pot, hash and coke – the "natural" stuff. I didn't drink beer or smoke pot because it spoiled my high on speed. Don't forget what years these were – days of "inner peace" and expanding one's mind with LSD and other hallucinogens, which we used almost every weekend.

In those days women in the construction trades did not exist. N.O.W. was being formed and "liberated" women were burning their bras and draft dodgers were burning their draft cards. These were very turbulent times. The country was on the move, but no one knew in what direction. One construction worker was overheard telling another one, "Those drywall finishers are crazy. Not only are they wearing their pants cut off, but they got their hair tied up in two ponytails!" They had no idea a woman was on the job. I wasn't looked upon as someone's "old lady", but rather my own person. I was one of the guys and I loved it! I had my own long-handled "wipe down" knife with my name carved in it.

After the first year, the word got back to the union that there was a woman in the trade. Union reps would cruise the job sites looking for me. Harry was against the union and would have me hide -- sometimes in a sweltering attic. The union was not out to help me, but to help themselves. By getting the first woman in the brotherhood, they could appease several political groups.

CHAPTER 19

After awhile we couldn't fight it anymore and we finally joined the union. It was exciting. I was the first woman in a union in Southern California. They crossed out "brother" and wrote "sister" Nanci on my union card. "Finally, some recognition," I thought.

Life was great. We were making good money. We bought a 1947 Harley "45", chopped. It was a pretty thing. This opened up a whole new door. Motorcycle shows, partying with bikers, rowdy parties, lots of drugs.

All along I knew I didn't want to pack behind someone, but wanted my own bike. In 1970 we bought "Babe". She was a 1969 Triumph Bonneville that had been raced. We had her rebuilt and she was beautiful. I'd take her for rides up in the mountains and she would just purr. Me and Babe. It was a release like I never felt before.

In 1971 a construction boom hit southern California and the town was rockin'. It was like the gold rush days; people were coming from all over to get a piece of the action. For three and one-half years we worked seven days a week. We were making so much money, with no deductions, that we were paying $300-$400 a week in taxes. We decided to buy some property. After a time of looking, we purchased "The Ranch". It was a five-bedroom ranch home on three acres just east of San Diego; it was great! We were working continually on the land – clearing it, watering lawns, pruning trees, installing fences and corrals. Hard work wasn't looked upon as work, but rather "performance for pleasure". It was a ticket for a trip in the "fast lane" -- drugs, Dobermans, horses, motorcycles, trucks and RV's. We were going to Vegas every three months to party. We got on the horses and headed across the street to a mountain range leading to the LA area. We would get on the bikes and putt up to Big Bear. More speed, more acid, more work, more money, on it went like a forceful tornado taking everything in its path to feed itself.

Harry was everything to me – a father figure, a friend and a lover. He was my god, having special power over my life -- to be honored and admired.

During these years I changed radically in my appearance. I exchanged the mini-dresses and "go-go" boots for jeans, white t-shirt and work boots. I became very muscular. I tied my hair up and never wore any makeup. I always had a tan. No jewelry except for a watch. One night I was shooting pool in a bar with a friend. I wore a "Tom Jones" shirt with a wide collar and blouson sleeves, jeans, boots and a long suede vest. My hair was cut in a shag and I wore "John Lennon" wire-framed glasses. A couple of guys asked me if I was a man or a woman. I sloughed it off as it being "their" problem. Little did I know how far my pendulum had swung away from being the woman God had designed and created.

There was always something to do on The Ranch. Taking the pups on a perimeter walk around the property, tying a horse to the exterior antenna for a "shoeing" or holding onto both horses while Harry saddled them for a ride. His horse was a little skittish and one time when I was standing between the two horses, Harry swung to hit his horse. Just as he did that, the horse reared up. Harry missed the horse and caught me in the jaw! I saw stars. My knees buckled and the horses reared up. What a way to start out on a ride! This was just an example of life on The Ranch; it was very physical.

CHAPTER 20

Someone had built a few tract homes across the street from us and the people that lived in them would sit in chairs in their driveways and watch us. "Why don't they get a life?" I thought.

Our living room furnishings were very different. In our first house we had a queen sized bed in the living room for four years! Meals were eaten off of TV trays and guests sat on the sides. I'm not quite sure why we did this; it just seemed to work. I didn't ask why because I was always told that I wasn't paid to think. My life was so full now of the things I always wanted – money, a job I loved and respect. I accepted the fact I didn't have to plan and maneuver life; just enjoy it.

One evening when we were in the front yard with the pups, a taxi cab pulled into our driveway. Being out in the country, I figured he was lost. As I looked at the passenger waving, I realized that it was my mother! She hadn't heard from me for a few years and decided to fly out from Boston to find me and see if I was alright. "Besides", she said, "if I didn't find you, at least I would get to see Southern California."

We got her a motel room and she stayed for a few days. One evening my mother and I were looking out at the panoramic view from the back side of the ranch, watching the sun starting to set. Harry was out at the corrals feeding the horses. My mother asked me, "Doesn't he want his supper now?" "We'll eat when we get around to it," I replied. She was so programmed for a dinner of "meat and potatoes" on the table promptly at 5:00 p.m., like all the other New England shipyard families, she couldn't conceive of so much flexibility. "Oh, Nanci," she said, "you live like so many people wish they could live." "That's right," I thought, "take that back to New England with you!" In all of my bitterness, I didn't realize until years later that it was she, herself, who wanted that freedom.

My mother was so overwhelmed by life that her ability to respond to stimulation was shot. She just "accepted" everything without saying a word. Now I see where I get it from! Like the first time she walked into the living room at the ranch. There was a dramatic ten foot wide fireplace mantle complete with stones from across the country. Two sofas back-to-back and "Babe", my motorcycle! Someone had stolen her beautiful tank one time so I kept her inside. Without a word about how unusual it was to have a motorcycle in the house, Mother walked in, sat down, and I began telling her all about what I've been doing with my life.

"Oh yeah," I said, I ride a motorcycle now." "That's nice," Mother replied.

"It's that one behind you," I told her.

She turned around and looked at it and smiled. She then did a double take and asked, "You ride that?"

"Yep, sure do," I replied.

"Take that story back to New England with you," I thought. I didn't realize why I had to be

an "over-comer", but I had to prove something --
to excel, to achieve. It was because of the
bitterness that was burning deep inside me. No
one was ever going to hold me down again.
Mother returned to Boston with a promise that I
would keep in touch.

Another interesting aspect of living with
Harry was the fact that we never celebrated
holidays, including Christmas and birthdays.
Too busy, "achieving", I guess. Life itself was one
big celebration. It was fun. It was alive, intense.
It was happening.

CHAPTER 21

This year wasn't just the "Fast Lane", it was the whole highway. After being together for several years Harry and I decided to get married. One day we polished our bikes, put on our good jeans, boots and custom-made vests and rode to a little wedding chapel in Mission Valley. No one was with us, just the JP and his wife as a witness. After the ten minute ceremony we went to a "friend's" house to get some coke. That was it for the wedding day.

It was 1974; a time when drugs poured across the Mexican border like a fast, flooded river. Being a woman in the drug culture was sort of like being a mob wife. You knew something was going on but "business" was never discussed with the women. Little did I know that while Harry and I were working in construction, he was building relationships of trust with the dealers. When we went over to the main house for an evening, after a time of food and fellowship and a lot of cocaine, the men would meet in a separate room while we women were cleaning up in the kitchen. I became friends with one of them. If I asked Harry anything that wasn't pertaining to our construction work, the cooking or the laundry, he would always respond with, "Lucille, you don't get paid to think." Because of that I was totally oblivious to the situation that was being created. He also made sure that I stayed busy and maintained a distance between me and the other wives.

Per pre-arranged plans, one night and Harry and I headed for Tijuana. The order of the day was: construction by day, fix supper after work, then go to Mexico for a drug deal. A deal went down and we were chosen to smuggle a shipment of 60,000 downers and uppers across the Mexican border to San Diego. I don't know why we did it. It wasn't like we needed the money. But I was with Harry and anything he did or said was fine by me! He was "the man". Since Harry was already on State probation for a previous drug violation, just in case we ever got busted we created and maintained a story that the "goods" in the back of his truck were mine; that he had picked me up in Tijuana, Mexico, and was giving me a ride back to the States.

Okay, so there we were in Mexico, waiting in the "contact's" office. For hours we sat in the dark, in silence while porn movies played. Finally the deal went down and we headed for the border with that shipment of downers and uppers hidden in the bed of our truck among work tools. It was a quiet week night with normal traffic to the States. We pulled up to the check point and the US Border Patrol began tearing everything apart in the back of the truck! They found all the "goods". I believe we were set up. We were separated in the Federal interrogation office and we both stuck to the story as planned.

We hired very expensive criminal attorneys that were successfully used by everyone we knew in the "business". Mine told me that I needed to bring my father out from D.C. as a character reference. "Oh no, I can't do that," I pleaded. He insisted that it would affect my sentence and keep me out of jail. My father had retired from the Air Force and was now at the FAA. I called him and he flew out and accompanied me to the court hearing. When the judge asked him if he had anything to say, he pointed to Harry and said, "Your Honor, this man is corrupting my daughter." What? This was the man I loved. How could he? I got two years probation and Harry got thirty days. Dad flew home.

CHAPTER 22

While Harry was in jail, I set out to find some work; to be someone's "Wipedown Man". I found out about a college kid that was stringing tape on a job so I went over there to see him. He had two guys wiping down behind him that didn't know what they were doing. I told him I was twice as fast as both those guys and he would only have to pay for me. He fired them on the spot and for the next thirty days I worked with this kid. I taught him a lot and saved a job for Harry. When Harry got out of jail he talked to the Super and moved in on the kid's job. That's just how we rolled.

Another thing that happened that year; I became the first woman journeyman drywall finisher and was voted in unanimously by the union members. It was one of the great highlights of my life. I had found myself! I had met myself! I liked who I was. I was invincible. I could do anything. I was stronger and faster than ever. Local newspapers called me for interviews. We were known all over San Diego County as the best drywall team around. Some of the high-priced custom contractors would only allow us to do their jobs. Life was good.

We heard from an old friend in the construction business. He called to check our availability. Seems he had a big condo job up in Carlsbad and was running behind schedule getting the tape on. When the sheetrock is up and finished, it's like one wall and the bank considers that point a phase where more money can be released. We decided that Harry would stay and finish our current job while I went up North to run this job and help out our friend. This would be the first job that I ran myself. Now remember, there were still NO women in the trades at this time. We got caught up and finished with minimal late fines. The general contractor came out everyday to check on things. He smoked cigars and called me "Sweetheart". I hated that. "He wouldn't have done that if Harry was here," I thought. Oh, well, after all I was in a man's world.

With these jobs finished, we started on a HUGE job of tract homes that was going to last for over three years. Everybody was on speed and we were flying! During the third year in Mira Mesa, we started that morning taping the cathedral ceiling in a big two-story house. I slipped in some mud while up on the scaffold and fell 17 feet onto concrete. I landed on my back and split my head open. Going down, I remember thinking, "This is the beginning of the end." I was so tough that I finished working that day! The next morning I couldn't move my legs. Harry took me to the Doctor's and x-rays showed that all my vertebrae were turned toward the front and my tail bone was cracked. I was taped up in a soft body cast and told to rest. When your adrenaline has been so high for so long it's hard to stop. I returned to work. The wrappings bothered me so I took them off and threw them in a ditch on the job and kept on going.

More changes came in the form of selling the beloved ranch. We got rid of the animals and Harry's bike and bought a three-year-old tract house nearby. Another loss. I loved the ranch. I thought it was home and I was home. Oh well, here we go again, nothing last forever.

My back wouldn't allow me to work in drywall anymore so we started a cleanup, hauling, landscaping business. During the first year in our new business, we sold that house. I don't know why and don't remember moving into the rental house; probably the drugs or I just blocked it out. It was nothing great, just going through the days. Harry was stressed over running the business. If I wasn't working in the kitchen, he made me stand by his desk in case he needed something. During this time he made me sell my bike – my beloved "Babe". I thought to myself, "He couldn't love me if he would do this." More loss.

Eventually we bought a brand new Dodge Ramcharger, put all our things in storage and set out on a three month cross-country trip to get away and visit our families.

CHAPTER 23

Harry and I started our trip by heading North up the wondrous Pacific Coast Highway to visit some friends in northern California. With the ocean on our left and towns like Del Mar, Laguna Niguel and Newport on our right, we savored the salt sea breezes, the warm California sunshine and the majestic views.

The first night we stayed in a motel right on the beach. The soothing sound of the surf lulled these weary road-warriors into a sweet sleep. We headed out early the next morning in order to get through Los Angeles before traffic got heavy. Grabbing some breakfast, we headed for Monterey. After seeing the beautiful surf and the flowers on the cliffs growing down to meet the beach, we both agreed that if there was a "heaven on earth" this was it.

We continued north to our friend's place just east of San Francisco. Hector and Gloria were homesteading 40 acres of raw land. They had built a huge barn and, while they slept in the loft upstairs, they shared the main room with their animals! They smoked great homegrown reefer, ate homemade cheese and drank fresh goat's milk which was always running down Hector's beard. Gloria owned a couple of vintage clothing stores in San Francisco and always wore a full-length mink coat. The two of them had a 25 foot flatbed truck with barrels and crates full of vintage clothes. Hector opened some of them and said, "Take what you want." We helped ourselves to some old baseball jerseys, coveralls and a variety of shirts.

Gloria and Hector were great hosts but after a few days it was time to move on. When they wanted to know where we were headed, Harry replied, "Yosemite". Gloria, knowing it would be cold up there, removed her mink coat and gave it to me. We said our goodbyes and headed East on another adventure. Shortly after our departure, we got the news that Hector had been decapitated while riding his Harley! A loaded lumber truck pulled too close in front of him.

Harry drove all night. I took over in the morning. As we changed seats Harry said, "If you see an animal standing in the road, don't swerve to the right or left as they will usually run. Hit it head on." Sure enough, while driving in the early morning mist, up the mountain to Yosemite, there was a big deer standing in the road. Harry was sleeping so I proceeded forward hoping the deer would move. It didn't and BLAM, I hit it! I explained to Harry what happened. He dragged it down into a ditch and put it out of its misery.

We checked into the rustic Yosemite ranger station and got our assigned campsite. It was right beneath majestic Half Dome, a rock so steep that it had never been scaled by man. We set up on a primitive campsite, hiked during the day and cuddled by the fire in the evening. Late at night we made love on the campsite picnic table, not caring who saw us. The mountain air breezes and the wind songs rustling through the trees seemed to wash away the debris of "Life in the Fast Lane". It was so good to laugh and just "be" after so many years in the fast lane. It didn't matter that Harry never told me he loved me. Just being with him was enough. What was in my head was that he was everything to me. The next morning after cooking breakfast over the open fire, we broke camp and headed for Arizona to find a campground a friend recommended.

"Lucille," Harry said, "Load us up; we're outta here".

CHAPTER 24

We arrived at what should have been the
Arizona campground that night, only to discover
that it no longer existed. Only the saguaros,
lizards and scorpions remained. So much for
following an old, outdated map. We made a fire,
cooked some supper, threw down our sleeping
bags and went to sleep. When we woke up, we
found ourselves covered head to toe with
tarantulas! We both jumped up and shook off
the innocent visitors. I fixed some coffee and
breakfast over a fire while Harry explored the
area.

Still trying to settle into a slower pace, we
decided to camp the next night in nearby New
Mexico. This was a State that we had not
camped in before. Uncharted territory – yippee!

Back in those days about the only traffic on
the desert roads during the week were the
truckers. We followed the desolate highway
across the Arizona desert, enjoying its beauty
and solitude. Arriving in New Mexico, we
stopped for supplies. I bought a disposable
camera. Shifting into 4-wheel drive, we headed
out to do some "off-roading". Eventually we came
upon a very interesting abandoned mine with
multi-colored smelting jars and an old liquor
bottle lying on the ground. The mine provided
cold air for the food cooler, so we set up camp
there.

We always enjoyed being close to Nature. The wind gusted up to welcome us. The high desert pinion trees swayed to show us which way the wind was blowing. We found an old wood and metal machine shop framed with 2x4's inside. It was just right for holding the canned goods. The concrete floor provided a place to sleep. The center of the floor had been removed and used as a fire pit. It was a perfect "Desert Inn" for these travelers. Every day there was something to explore. The first day we went down into the mine shaft and got lost in one of the turns on the way out. The next day we tied string to the front entrance to carry with us, providing a safe return. We also wore our winter jackets as the air in the mine was very cold. We found more smelting cups that the miners had used to separate out the gold. They were made of pottery about the size of a coffee mug; layers of magnificent colors had been baked inside them during the smelting process.

On the third night of our stay there, a very strange thing happened! The moon was full. We did not build a fire. We settled into our sleeping bags for a night's sleep. In the middle of the night Harry was awakened by the heat of his sleeping bag -- it was burning up around him! The stainless steel pistol he had with him got hot too. We took this strange happening as a sign to move on. The next morning we packed up, took pictures of the remains of the burned up sleeping bag and headed for Harry's sister's place in Colorado.

CHAPTER 25

Even though we were surrounded by the beauty and serenity of the Southwest, everything seemed surreal to me. The ranch was gone, the horses were gone, the dogs were gone. Our jobs were gone and sometimes I wondered where we were going and why. I wondered if we were sojourners on the run, or if we were just trying to rebuild our relationship.

The highway brought us to beautiful Colorado Springs, Colorado. Harry's sister was the youngest of the five sisters; Harry was the youngest of all nine children. Patty and her husband, Alex, lived in a lovely log home that was heated by the local hot springs. They told us that you could even go "tubing" in the warm waters of the hot springs in the winter months when everything else was frozen... a winter sport besides skiing!

While in their home, we sensed a lot of darkness and sadness. We kept our visit short— we had some good food, hot showers and headed on to see Harry's oldest brother, Will, and his family. They lived near the original family homestead in Dumas, Texas. Harry's mother was a Cherokee and his father was Irish. Thus all the kids were good looking, high-spirited and loved to dance. Will was a preacher in the Bible belt and also had a band. All of Harry's family were musically gifted; some had developed their talent more than others.

We were greeted warmly and had some great conversations over dinner about where everybody was and what they were doing. Harry enjoyed sharing this even though he had been estranged from the family for many years. When we went to bed that night, he told me, "They don't believe we are married because we're wearing turquoise wedding bands." We kept that visit short also, and soon found ourselves on the road to Arkansas to visit another of Harry's sisters.

CHAPTER 26

Greenbriar, Arkansas! What fun! Family, football and chocolate gravy! Bob, the brother-in-law, was the mayor of this wonderful country town. Ann, Harry's sister, was a typical Texas girl—good looking and charming. They had two daughters and one son.

We were still taking speed every day, smoking cigarillos and having a blast with this fun-loving family. One morning at breakfast I asked if there were any abandoned farms in the area that might have some old bottles lying around. "Yes, I know where there is one," replied Claire, the youngest daughter. "Okay, let's go find it," Harry said. Harry, Claire and I traveled down a dirt road for awhile until we came to a "moonshine bridge". For those of you who don't know what that is, it is two planks thrown across a ravine. You have to be crazy or desperate to drive over it. I guess we were crazy because over it we went. It felt like the old days to us, fearless and free. We had to park the truck as the house and barn were in the middle of a huge forest of trees and tall grass that had grown up around the buildings. We were walking swiftly when, BAM! I ran into forehead-high barbed wire and ripped open my forehead. I put a bandana on it and kept on going. Finally we got to the barn. "Oh, my gosh," I spouted. There, just sitting on the 2x4 ribs of the barn, were lots and lots of canning jars. They were empty and it was as if they were waiting for us to come and rescue them. After gathering and loading these wonderful treasures in the truck, we headed for the house to see what was inside. It was as if the entire family just up and left – very eerie. The furniture was still in place and there were frayed curtains on the windows. They say these farms were abandoned during the Dust Bowl of the 1930's. It was now the 1970's. People hadn't gotten into treasure hunting in such remote places yet. Checking for rats or mice, we slowly pulled the stove out from the wall and discovered two beautifully faceted jelly jars. We were having so much fun that we didn't realize the day had gone by. Hunger was the only reminder.

We decided to take another way back that would be longer but safer. By nightfall we were totally lost in the middle of Nowhere, Arkansas. We came upon a small cabin. I got out and knocked on the door of this dark, creepy, haunted-looking cabin. The door was slowly opened by a tall thin man wearing a dirty undershirt and missing an eye. As I tried to ask for directions, my eyes caught those of a woman. She had long black hair, dark clothes and she was sitting on the floor by the fire, stirring a pot of something. She looked like a witch. I'm sure he gave me directions, but to this day I cannot recall them! I guess we made it back because the next day was Friday, which meant the high school football game; Harry's nephew was on the team. The whole town showed up. What fun we had in this all-American town full of warm, friendly people. Okay, time to get on the road.

CHAPTER 27

As we headed east to see my Dad in Washington, D.C., we cruised down the highway listening to Credence Clearwater Revival, Santana and Pink Floyd. Life was good. Dad had been married to my step-mother, Maxine, for 20 years. She was a hoot and a true match for Dad. She was very out-going; totally opposite from my biological mother who was a refined introvert. Dad retired from 22 years in the Air Force and went to work for the FAA as an engineer on the Concord team. Maxine worked as a telephone operator for the Smithsonian for 30 years.

It was October of 1975. The worst of that year was the Watergate Scandal. The best was Bill Gates founding Microsoft in New Mexico. Some of the highlights from that year included beginning construction of the Alaskan Pipeline, the "Thrilla in Manila" when Mohammad Ali defeated Joe Frazier, and of course, the first episode of Saturday Night Live hosted by George Carlin.

We had a great visit while in D.C., even a private tour of the Smithsonian. Wow! I liked the Wright Bros. plane and Fonzie's leather jacket. We wanted to tour the White House but the flag on it was flying which meant that President Ford was there and no tours were allowed.

Dad and Harry got along well considering the things my Dad had said about him when he flew out to testify for me at a court hearing for the drug bust a few years earlier. I think Dad just accepted the fact that I really loved this guy and he wasn't going anywhere. We stayed for a few days with the partying beer drinkers. Soon we said our goodbyes and headed north to Boston to see my mother.

As soon as we arrived in Massachusetts I felt that eerie, heavy darkness again; just like in Colorado.

My daughters were now nine and ten years old. The woman who took them away from me (Sven's mother) allowed them to visit me at my mother's house. They were just darling! We ate, talked and took pictures. Saying goodbye was difficult. I wouldn't see them again for another ten years. The next day we went to my sister's for dinner. She said she vividly remembers when she called everyone to come and eat. Harry put his gun on the table and sat down! I have no idea why he did that except to intimidate the men in the house. After that visit to my sister's, we headed west. I felt very detached from my family and I was happy to be on the road back toward "home" even though we didn't have one.

CHAPTER 28

We took a different route back and traveled through the Midwest, Kansas, New Mexico and back to California. Most of our stops were made in very secluded, desolate areas like mine shafts or huge corn fields. Sometimes an eerie feeling would come over me when we were in those places. While fixing some sandwiches or just resting, I became aware of a very evil feeling, the creepy feeling one gets when watching a scary movie. It would get very quiet and I would sense that Harry was thinking of killing me. I didn't know why I was feeling like this but it happened on several occasions during our trip.

We were within shouting distance of our friends' place in San Diego so we stopped to visit them. Sadie and Benny had sold us our horses. As we talked over old times, we discovered that a mutual friend and nearby rancher, Ozzie, was dying of bone cancer and needed help. Harry and I went to see him and told him we would stay at his ranch and care for him for as long as he needed us. Harry went back to work in construction while I cared for Ozzie and his animals. This was a depressing time for me. I was no long excited about each day. I felt lost with no direction. As each day passed with Ozzie getting closer to his death, I felt there was something inside of me that was dying also. Ozzie's suffering finally came to an end. His family was notified and we had to find another place to live.

Another horse person named Crystal opened her home to us, so we stayed there with her and her boyfriend, a handsome sailor named Hank. Things just weren't feeling right to me anymore. I couldn't understand why we didn't get an apartment and take our stuff out of storage. I kept waiting every day for Harry to create something and lead us out of there, but he never did. I knew that Crystal really liked Harry and wanted me out of the way. We were doing a lot of partying with drugs and reefer. One night Hank told me that he was being transferred to Memphis next week and did I want to go with him. There had been four months of living out of a suitcase and I had had it with Harry. "Yes," I replied, "I'll go with you since I'm already packed." As we backed out of the driveway the next day, Harry stood at the front door and hollered to me, "You're making a mistake." I replied, "You're probably right but I gotta go." It wasn't until years later that I realized this was a plan of Crystal's and Hank's to get rid of me.

When we arrived in Memphis we stopped in a bar for a beer. The owner said, "I need a barmaid tonight; want a job?" "Sure," I said, "Let me get unpacked and I'll be right back." Hank turned out to be a total asshole; so were the bar customers. Weeks passed; I was tired of the crap. I packed my suitcase, got a ride to the highway and was hitchhiking back to San Diego when a trucker stopped and picked me up. I traveled with him to Los Angeles where he dropped off his load. I was enjoying his company and being away from everything while on the road. I stayed with him and on the way back East, he said he would leave me in Memphis where I could easily get a CDL license and then travel with him. He said he would pick me up on the way back. I got the license but he never did return. At this time I was staying with a gal who had been my neighbor. When I told her of my plight she said, "I'll go with you to San Diego. I have a brand new Mustang!" "Come on," I replied, and off we went.

When we arrived in San Diego, Sherri and I rented a small furnished house. She went to work as a waitress and I went back to work with Harry. We were making good money again and life was fun. My back was healed and it was good to be back to work, not to mention being back with Harry, even though he was still living with Crystal.

One night Sherri asked me to take her to T.J. "I want to see Tijuana," she said. We headed south to Mexico and wound up meeting two brothers that we partied with down there every weekend for about six weeks. Sherri decided she was going back to Memphis. In the meantime, since I hadn't been feeling too good, I decided to go to see a doctor. Tests showed that I was pregnant! "Oh, NO," I thought, "this can't be." Harry had had a vasectomy and I didn't even know where to find the guy in Mexico. Should I have another abortion? That way no one would ever know. I felt abandoned and, again, all alone.

CHAPTER 29

I call this part of my life Bitter-Sweet. It was bitter because everything I loved and cherished was gone: my relationship with Harry, my career, the beloved ranch, the dogs, the horses and my motorcycle. Everything I identified with was gone. The sweet part was that I was pregnant and now I had a chance to start my life in California fresh and new. I signed up for welfare and moved across town away from all my drug-using "friends" and embarked on this new adventure.

After a couple of months a drug lord found out that I was in town and available to help him. (So much for leaving my drug friends.) Knowing that he could trust me made me an asset. He contacted me and offered to let me stay rent free in a large house that he and his wife had for sale. I figured this would allow me to save up some money for baby items. "How nice," I thought, "they want to help me." They moved me in and I set up my house. I walked two miles every day, made homemade soups and thought good thoughts. Although these were the days before ultra-sound, I was sure I was carrying a male child. What should I name him? If he was going to run with me, he would be on a lot of adventures, so I named him Jason, after Jason and the Argonauts. According to the legend, they were always involved in an adventure and

Jason, their leader, overcame many obstacles and survived as a hero.

Everything was going very well until the drug lord contacted me. He said that a dealer was coming into town from out of state and he wanted me to put him up at the house. I couldn't say "no" because it was his house. No one could know how long it would take for a connection to be made and the deal to go down. It depended on the contacts in Mexico. It could be two hours or two days. The dealer arrived and went into the bathroom, locked the door, got high on something, stayed in there all night and beat up the bathroom. The next morning the deal was done and he was gone. This was considered a "smooth deal". As time went on I continued to host "visitors" but I did not like it.

By now it was December and I was contacted by the drug lord and asked to fly 18 kilos of marijuana into a town in Wyoming for him. I accepted the job because it would give me enough money to rent my own place and get away from all of this once and for all. I went over to the dealer's house. He gave me some counterfeit 100 hundred dollar bills and told me to get some luggage to carry the shipment. Thank God bills were not checked in those days because OFAMERICA was all one word! I returned with the luggage. The dealers lined it with foil, foil-wrapped each kilo, gave me an airline ticket and some cash. That same drug lord had someone drive me to the airport and as I was leaving he said to me, "If there's a bust just walk away."

As we were making our descent at the little airport in No-Where, Wyoming, I could see the local sheriff sitting by a window having coffee in what was the airport terminal. It looked like a log cabin. "I'm busted, this will never go through security," I thought. Somehow it did go through; my contacts were two dealers I knew from San Diego. They put the suitcases in the bed of the truck and the three of us headed for the contact's place. We were traveling towards downtown when, at an intersection, four cop cars came in from all directions and surrounded us. While their guns were drawn on us, I had a vision of having my baby in prison. They pulled the two guys out from each side of the truck cab. I got out on my own and one of the officers turned to me and said, "There is a pay phone over there in the bar if you need to call someone," and pointed up the street. I thanked him and walked calmly to the back door of the bar. Once inside I leaned up against a wall and tried to catch my breath. "What just happened?" I wondered. "Why did they bust them and not me?" I did not realize until years later that I was being protected by the spirit realm because I couldn't protect myself at the time.

I called the contact person there and he came and got me. I had to spend the night on a porch with no heat in December in Wyoming. The next morning he took me out of the State and I flew home from Billings, Montana. This was the first of many adventures that my son and I would go on together.

CHAPTER 30

I did not realize until years later how much
of my power I had given away to people that
didn't deserve it. However I have learned that
everyone and everything that comes into our
lives is here to teach us something. This terrible
life style would eventually drive me to seek the
Truth and for that I am grateful.

Once again I moved, this time into a duplex
that I shared with a lovely young Navy couple.
On June 25, 1977, I gave birth to a handsome
baby boy. Jason was finally here with me. I had
something to live for but because of bad choices
my life just wouldn't change.

I returned to work in construction a couple
more times on my own. Male chauvinism was
rampant in those days especially in
construction. They did not want a woman on the
job even though I had been in the trades for
years and was a journeyman. After episodes like
all the drywall mud that I needed was hidden, I
decided that this season of my life was over and
it was time to make a major change.

When Jason was 18 months old I found a
wonderful Christian babysitter. That enabled me
to enroll in Beauty College. My dream was
coming true! I needed some support while in
school. There was a guy from the local bar that
liked me so I invited him to move in with Jason
and me. He worked as a chef and paid all of the

bills while I went to school. I didn't care about anybody except my Jason, and making a life for the two of us. As soon as I graduated I dumped the guy. I got a job in a salon where I was a star and found a new apartment. Life was great! My life was doing hair and partying. I was hot. I was on my way back "up" again. No one was ever going to hurt me again. Hair shows, competitions and Mob related parties; back to life in the fast lane.

I did manage to connect with Jason's father in Mexico and for the next six years I brought Jason down to his grandmother's one weekend every month. I wanted him to know his culture and his family. He also spent a lot of time at the babysitters.

Four years passed. It was 1984. Jason's father got married and didn't want Jason to visit anymore. My boss announced he was selling the salon and I found myself broke, homeless, hopeless and fried from all the partying. I was evicted from my apartment.

CHAPTER 31

My son and I were living in an ant-infested tent for several weeks. The local grocery store where I picked up food for us everyday had a bingo game going. The prize was $2500 and I only needed one more ticket. Since I was still working at the salon part time, I put an ad in the paper. "Need Big Bear Market Bingo number B5. Will split the prize." I figured $1250 would be enough for us to get an apartment. The next day I got a call at the salon from a guy who said he was an airline pilot. I could keep all the money and did I want to meet him. "Sure," I said with great excitement. He told me to come to a motel in El Cajon at 7:00 p.m. I fed Jason and told him to stay there in the tent until I got back. He was so good, I never had to worry about him straying away even though he was only six years old.

I knocked on the guy's motel room door. I was so out of it that when he opened it I didn't realize that airline pilots don't have long white beards. I entered his room and he told me that all he wanted for the ticket was some good sex. "Okay," I said. No problem I thought.

When we were finished he held me in his arms and said "I really like you, Nanci, and I would like to take care of you and your son. I will give you a check right now for the whole $2500, and I will give you that much every month and you won't have to worry about anything."

I said, "Okay". We got dressed and he wrote me a check. He told me to go and get a nice apartment and call him when I was settled. I couldn't sleep that night. I got up early; Jason and I went to the bank before it opened the next morning. When I presented the check and my I.D. to the teller, she looked at the check and said, "This is a bogus check." She called the number on it and a guy from the Pizza Hut answered. It was at that moment I literally went "over the rainbow".

Somehow I managed to get a job at a local business that had a lot of cash running through it all day long. There was a "drop safe" in the floor and on my second day there, I lined it with a cloth bag. I hit all the wrong amounts on the register during my shift so they wouldn't know how much money I took. I removed the bag, put it in my purse, and ended my shift.

I knew that I would have to get out of town right away. I called a friend of mine who was the president of a motorcycle gang. I told him that I needed some guys posted at a U-Haul to rent me a truck and some other guys at the storage place where my stuff was. I was loaded up with a bag of cocaine and a bowie knife under the seat. My car was loaded onto a dolly behind the truck. I didn't stop driving until I crossed the Mississippi River. I headed for my sister's in Boston.

CHAPTER 32

It took Jason and me a week in that U-Haul truck to get across America. On the seventh morning we arrived at my sister's place in Pembroke, Massachusetts. As I carefully pulled the truck down their long country driveway, I saw that my whole family was there to welcome me! Even my dad and stepmom came up. It was good to see everyone. It was a chilly October. My brother-in-law made a crackling fire in the fireplace. I had hot mulled cider and my sister made my favorite dish, lasagna. Everyone knew that I was at the end of my rope emotionally, spiritually and physically; that it would take something this big for me to leave my beloved California.

I want to share this with you because even though I was surrounded by all of this love and support, I couldn't feel it. I was numb and unaware. However, God is love and love never fails; it just blossoms at different times, that's all.

I enrolled Jason in school and now it remained for me to find a job. A high school friend of mine, Maryann, was a supervisor for the Defense Department in Boston. "Why don't you take the Civil Service test and come to work with me?" she suggested. "No thanks," I replied, "I want to work as a hairdresser." I considered the pros and cons of her offer that night. After I dropped Jason off at school the next morning, I grabbed a subway to Boston and took the Civil Service test.

I did pass the test in good form and started working at the Defense Department. I arranged to have payroll deductions to Children's United Way for the next three years to pay back the money I had stolen. I rented a house in a small town in the country for Jason and me. It was a typical New England town – the local sheriff was the Boy Scout Master, there was ice skating on the frozen pond in the winter, swimming in the lake in summer. Life was good.

Soon I was promoted to Department head over eight clerks. Working in an office and managing people was difficult for me. Consequently over the next five years I took enough valium everyday to tranquilize an elephant. The valium, along with coke and wine at night allowed me to "cope". In my spirit I was still at a dead end.

During my third Christmas in Massachusetts I invited a guy named Buddy to move in with us. We worked together. Buddy liked me and he liked Jason. This helped with the finances. I soon discovered that he was an alcoholic, drinking a fifth of VO everyday.

Between the commute into Boston, the job and this relationship, I was on overload again. I decided to transfer to the local Naval Air Station. It was right near my house, casual dress and a no-stress job counting nuts and bolts.

There was an extremely funny Marine gunny sergeant, Farley, who stopped by everyday. I couldn't understand why everyone turned away from him when he talked about God. I didn't have a problem talking about God. After all, my Christian Scientist mother raised me knowing "God is Love".

Time passed and Farley and I developed a rapport. Through the haze of valium and coke, I didn't realize that I was his "assignment". Nor did I realize that his wife just "happened" to stop by one day to invite me to go with them to a concert at their church later that week. I said, "Sure, why not?" I was happy to go as little Nanci was screaming for help.

When I got home that night, Buddy was so wasted that he could hardly drive Jason home from the ball park. "That's it," I thought. I've got to get rid of this guy even though I loved him. I went to work the next morning and told my boss that I needed the afternoon off. I also told Gunny that I couldn't make it to church; that I had something I had to take care of. All of a sudden he straightened up into the Marine stance and said to me sternly, "My wife and I are coming to pick you and your son up; if you're not ready, you're going to look awfully funny sitting there in that pew in your nightgown!" I knew he meant it. I said, "Okay, we'll be ready." So I went home from work and threw all of Buddy's stuff out, hoping that Farley and his wife would arrive while Buddy was there; they did. That week, Buddy, Jason and I all became born-again Christians in a little Baptist church near the beach. Buddy checked into a 30-day program at the VA hospital for his alcoholism. While in there, during my visits, he would say things like,

"Did you see how green the grass is today?" I would look out onto the greens and they looked the same to me. During another visit he would say, "Look how blue the sky is," with a new twinkle in his eye. He had no withdrawal symptoms and the result of a CAT scan revealed that he had the liver of a baby. Eventually we came to realize that he had a total miracle of deliverance. No desire to drink, he couldn't even remember what the stuff tasted like!

CHAPTER 33

I waited for the Lord, and he heard my cry;
He pulled me up from the miry pit, He set me on
the Rock.
He put a new song in my heart...
He set my goings upon a new path,
Many shall see and worship and put their trust in
the Lord.

Psalm 40

Now it was MY turn to get off the drugs. The next eight years were a time of restoration, and recovery – physically, emotionally and spiritually. Buddy and I got married and were transferred by the Department of Defense to Columbus, Ohio. My life was filled with frequent trips to the mental health and rehab facilities. After a few stays in one certain facility, I noticed that I felt a little better. The "darkness" was lighter. This particular facility was situated on a beautiful property with large oak trees that swayed on a breeze of love. After morning classes, we were allowed to choose how we would spend our afternoon. I chose to help in the garden. I walked down the musty smelling path each day to the garden with great anticipation. The pain seemed to go away while I was there. The couple that were the caretakers were very kind and nurturing. I enjoyed helping in the vegetable and herb gardens but the thing I liked most was playing with the lop-eared bunnies. They were so soft and cuddly, little Nanci liked them too.

During each visit to the facility I was allowed to take cuttings from a variety of plants and soon my living room at home was full of all sorts of greenery. I realized that I could replicate the natural environment that had helped me heal. Of course this meant I needed a bunny also. I added Oliver to the household. The love of nature that had been instilled in me as a child was blossoming, once again, from the inside out.

Another physical issue I had to address was severe damage to my nervous system from the drugs. I had to read a giant print Bible slowly because of the damage I had done to my optic nerve and brain function. This was the only way I could absorb and process what the Bible said. I also had continuous full body shakes that no one could see.

I knew I needed help and found two wonderful sources. The first was the local health food store. Because I was unable to work, our budget was tight. Even though I couldn't afford to buy any supplements, I would go to the store and read the books on healing the nervous system. I learned that Vitamin B complex was most important. So I bought foods rich in "B" and eventually got some supplements as well.

The other helpful source was a Christian book store on Main Street in the little town where we lived. One dark cloudy day I was very sad. I drove uptown where the little shops were and sat in my car crying. I cried a lot, maybe a river. I looked out my window and saw the sign, "Christian Book Store". I dried my bloodshot eyes and went in. It was very quiet and peaceful with soft music playing. I was greeted by the owner, a lovely lady named Tara. I cried again as I told her that we were new in town, that I was battling depression and I had no money to buy anything. She said, "Come see the videos I have for rent." We walked into a backroom and she loaded me up with quality movies, saying, "Your husband will like this one," and "Your son will love this one." No deposit, no I.D. I left with a stack of love and a, "I'll see you in a few days," from Tara. I believe that if you open your heart, God will send you what you need.

We joined the local Baptist Church where I enjoyed working with the preteen girls, hoping to sow something into them that would keep them off the streets. I joined a weekly Bible study. I only listened to Christian radio or watched Christian TV programs. I severed myself from the "world" and surrounded myself with only the good.

At night Buddy couldn't understand why I didn't want to watch shows like Miami Vice. I replied, "Why would I put something in front of me that is behind me?" This is when I started going to bed early and waking up to the next "Present".

CHAPTER 34

Even though Buddy and I put Jason into a Christian high school, we still had a hard time during his teen years. At one point, we were both in the same mental health facility at the same time. Poor Buddy. I remember one time we went for counseling about Jason while I was in a haze from all the anti-psychotic drugs they were giving me. I was on eight different medications. I couldn't function. It was hell all over again from street drugs to prescription drugs with the same dose of hopelessness.

We signed for Jason to join the Air Force when he was seventeen. The night before he was shipping out for boot camp I got on my knees at the end of my bed and prayed, "Dear Lord, I turn my son over to you to watch over him." Jason left and I had such peace in my heart. I thought, "Gee, this prayer stuff really works."

The next morning I got on my knees again at the end of my bed. I cried out to God, "I can't take this shaking one more day." The shaking disappeared instantly – up and out of my body. It was then that I knew I was going to be okay. Eventually the anxiety went away, the depression went away and I found a naturopath to help wean me off the drugs and replace them with natural substances.

It was during this time that I found Women's Aglow International. I heard on the radio that they were having a luncheon downtown to kick off a program that ministered to inner-city women. "Wow," I thought when I heard it, "This is what I'm supposed to do!" I contacted them and went to the luncheon. For the next four years I was their inner-city liaison. I absolutely loved ministering God's love to these precious women and encouraging them that they could "make it through" as I had. I also enjoyed speaking at the Aglow chapter meetings, telling these lovely ladies to never give up on these inner-city women. I told them how people had prayed for me for years with no signs of anything changing, yet their faith in God kept them going. I explained that they must keep their faith stirred up, to know that they were truly touching the hearts of the inner city women that came to the luncheons. I soon joined the non-denominational inner-city church where the luncheons were held. Buddy wanted to stay at the Baptist church which was fine.

For the next seven years I collected needed items for the women, helped feed 1800 homeless at Thanksgiving, helped with the Christmas program, started a bus ministry and created a fund-raising drive that outfitted our kids for camp each summer. Buddy sensed the excitement and joined in after about a year.

In 2000 Jason was out of the Air Force, married, living in Phoenix, Arizona, and my granddaughter, Jazmyn, was born. Even though my life in Columbus, Ohio, was full, I longed to be back out West with Jason and his family. Even though my daughters had children in New England, I wasn't close to them. I wanted to bond with this granddaughter before she got too old.

CHAPTER 35

In 2003, we had a huge going away party and moved to Tempe, Arizona. We leased an apartment while we built a house. Because all the "busy-ness" of life in Ohio was gone, I sensed an emptiness inside of me that I hadn't felt in a long time. Maybe that's why so many people stay busy; as a distraction from dealing with the Truth.

We moved into the new house, but I wasn't happy. I was grateful to Buddy for all that he had done for Jason and myself, knowing that he, too, had grown during the last fifteen years. I had come so far I didn't want to stop.

One time while I was in Scottsdale, I stumbled across an interesting bookstore. Maybe another "haven of help," I thought. As I entered I saw a strikingly handsome Native American man sitting at a table by the window. He had silver shoulder-length hair and was wearing one of those bone choker-style necklaces. I asked the shop owner, "Who is that?" "His name is Serge Running Wolf" she replied. "Can I speak with him?" I inquired. "Yes," she answered, "as soon as he is finished with his client." Oh, the feeling in that store was soooo wonderful: incense, soft music, colors, books and light.

When Serge was finished, I sat down at the table

with him. He told me that I needed to spend more time outdoors. He suggested that I take a trip to the Rio Verde River and come back to let him know what messages I got while up there. I thanked him, paid him some money and left.

One day I followed his directions and headed to the river. I found a dirt road and turned onto it. I drove slowly over the ruts and suddenly it was as though Spirit waved a hand and everything became "enchanted". Colors were very intense and vivid. A herd of wild horses ran by, led by a white one that turned and looked at me. I was awestruck. Abruptly, the road ended. As I got out and walked, I started to cry. It was July in the desert; I was in the middle of nowhere and I couldn't find the river.

All of a sudden a bird began chirping wildly in a tree as if to say, "It's this way." "Okay, I'm game," I thought. I followed this bird as he jumped from tree to tree. I could finally hear the rapids and felt the draw of the river. I took off my shoes and waded in.

The water was so cool and refreshing. Soft rapids sang to me. Knowing there was no one around, except for nature, I stripped down to my underwear and went into the river. As I lay on my back with arms outstretched, I asked the river to please baptize me. I don't know how long I lay there as the clear, bubbling water washed all my cares and concerns away. I felt so peaceful. Eventually I went to the shoreline where the water was warm and shallow. I settled down on my stomach and took a nap. I recalled the 23rd

Psalm: "He leads me beside the still waters; He restores my soul."

When I left I turned to river and said, "Thank you." When I got home I called Serge and told him I didn't really get any messages, but I did see a band of wild horses, and a bird that led me to the river. He said, "Those WERE the messages." and told me to keep going to the river as often as possible.

It is at this time that I left Buddy, bought an RV and moved up to the mountains in northern Arizona. I divorced Buddy. I had come so far I didn't want to stop. I wanted to be alone with God for the first time in my life. My son's German Shepherd adopted me and I brought him with me. I left the church. I left my life. I left my identity. For the next two years I just "was". Just listening.

CHAPTER 36

I began to realize that during my lifelong
quest for male love and acceptance I opened
myself up to threads of deception. They had
woven themselves into a blanket of invisible lies
that were smothering my soul. I knew they
needed to be washed away so I could be free of it
once and for all and transform the pain into self-
love. Nature became the oxygen for my body. I
allowed myself to be sustained and restored by
Nature. I realized that just like the majestic
eagle of the air, the fish of the river, the cool
grasses and even the rocks, I had a beautiful
purpose; not one of strife but of love. Each one
of us has his own divine path and purpose. The
important thing is to always stay on your path
by being true to yourself. You need to love
yourself first.

I would go for long walks and bask in the
beauty and harmony of the Creator. The warm
sun on my face, the quietness, a sunrise, or a
soft breeze – each one worked its magic. Soon I
became one with Nature. By that I mean I finally
saw in the spiritual mirror that I too was created
in beauty and harmony; that I was just as divine
as the eagles and hawks that I loved to watch. I
immersed myself daily in a bath of truth and
love. I knew that I did have a purpose -- one of
peace, love and joy.

My true identity began to emerge. I had the

same feeling that I had as a kid in the dog sled; that this "Now" feeling is true and right. I realized that I was finally off the "Merry-Go-Round". I truly was on a "Journey of Love". The other words that came to me during this time were, "Be still and know that I am God." This told me that what I was doing was okay. I could be still in my spirit. The chaos could be still. The chatter in my mind could be still. The worry could be still. The bitterness could be still.

I knew that I was home and little Nanci was free. Because my mind had changed, I was in the Promised Land of the Christ consciousness. Eventually my dog and I moved back down to the Valley. I rented a mobile home and got a job. I felt great. I did everything with love for myself first, then peace, then joy. My day was like a marching cadence, love, peace, joy, love, peace, joy, love, peace, joy. My boss's name was Harmony, so I threw that in there too. Each morning, almost child-like I would say to myself, "Today I walk in love of myself, peace, joy and harmony. Soon I added gratitude. Time passed and the places in my soul that were healed were now covered with a soft layer of profound love for others. I had confidence. I could smile at someone in a store; crazy drivers didn't steal my joy anymore. My identity was and is governed by love, peace, joy, harmony and gratitude. There is a lot of talk today about Identity Theft, but the ultimate Identity Theft happens when you allow someone or something to take you off your path of divine love.

I took frequent trips to camp at the river. I was allowing myself to be truly guided by a spiritual cloud of love by day, and a pillar of spiritual cleansing fire by night. What fun! What peace! What joy! My heart soared. A Native American musician once told me that we have a built in GPS guidance system and that it is very simple. If something makes your heart soar, embrace it. If it doesn't, walk away. A simple truth like that can go a long way toward helping a person along his or her spiritual path.

Except for visits and holidays with my wonderful son and granddaughter, I had been pretty much alone during those two years. Back again in the Valley I made friends with a new neighbor, Christina, and would have her over for supper when I cooked something special. She also had great joy and we laughed a lot.

We had a lot in common. We were both women and we were both Christians following our spiritual paths. This allowed us to talk and share about many things. One day she invited me to her church on Sunday. I was leery of experiencing another "Path Hijacking". I thought about it for a couple of days and finally agreed to go with her. I truly believe that when you are ready, your next teacher shows up.

We arrived late and service had already started. As we walked down the aisle, I noticed a picture of Jesus; but there was also a Buddha, some candles, beautiful colors and stars. It was as if this church embraced everything that was good. We sat in a middle row. The speaker was lovely. She was petite with short silver-grey hair and a dress that sparkled. She had a soft voice and the more she talked, the more she glowed.

I could tell that my spirit was being fed the

truth by the way I felt. My heart soared. I knew that I had found my spiritual home. She was the "Missing Link" that I had been looking for. As she spoke I thought, "As long as it feels right I'm going to keep coming here." I am now a member of that wonderful church. You see, religion is man-made while spirituality is God-made. So there has to be a link, a bridge that connects the two. The fabulous bridge that connects these is your mind. This is spiritual Christianity, the Christ consciousness. Here is where the rubber meets the road, my friend. This is when you use your built-in guidance system. If these truths make your heart soar, allow you to hear the birds' singing, smell a cup of coffee, smile about something, then keep on reading. If it doesn't, then close the book and do something else because we are going on the greatest journey of them all... finding your true self.

CHAPTER 37

I was very happy that I had made great strides in healing myself. Now it was time to fill in the empty spaces. My minister and my church were my new teachers. I attended church regularly and through my minister's teachings on God's love and Truth, I started to remember who I am. A deep joy rose up from within me and I became aware that I AM joy. Peace came up from within me and I became aware that I AM peace. Love came up from inside of me and I remembered that I AM love. I am my mirror and I can look at my reflection clearly and love myself. This is Divine love. Time passed and I remembered that I AM forgiveness and I could forgive myself and others. I could replace the lies told about me with God's love. I could replace the guilt and shame with God's truth about me. Most of all, I could replace the hopelessness with scripture. Mine was Philippians 4:13 (NIV) "I can do all things through Christ who strengthens me." All misconceptions and wrong thinking have gone away. I affirm that the Spirit of God that raised up Jesus dwells in me and I, like you, am the "Face of God".

I was like a plant blossoming -- a petal of patience, a leaf of mercy, a stem of righteousness and a petal of kindness. It didn't matter what was happening at the time, it was as if I was floating down the "River of Life."

Sometimes the water was still and quiet and other times it was strong and rushing. No matter what, I knew I was part of the Divine creation and I would be okay.

Just like the Israelites, God was still leading me through and to a Divine plan for my Highest Good. This was a time to remember. Jesus said, "You will know the truth and the truth will set you free." What was he talking about? For me it meant knowing the truth of who I am and being willing to be set free.

You want to get off the merry-go-round but don't know how. That's such a scary place. Even if you do manage to fall off all you can do is look backwards. Night and day, hot & cold, colors, black and white, fast or slow, smells good or bad -- it stays the same until you change your mind. You'll change your mind when you get tired of always looking at the same mess.

When you can change your mind you are home free. You've made it to the Promised Land! That's where a state of awareness, not numbness enters in.

This is the second coming of Christ that the Bible talks about. A new awareness of my Divine call and a birth into my own awakened Christ Consciousness. In Proverbs 23:7 the Bible says, "As we think, so we are."

I started intentionally thinking new thoughts about my situations. I began creating new horizons in my mind and in my world. Everything starts with a thought. It became most important to me to direct my "awareness" to my thoughts. I constantly monitored them. As I practiced I became more efficient at identifying wrong thoughts, casting them out and focusing on true thoughts.

There are two scriptures that helped me with this process and I would say them out loud all throughout the day. The first one was, "Phillipians 4:8 "Whatever is true, pure, honest, lovely and a good report, think on these things." The second scripture was, 1st Corinthians 2:16 which tells us "I cannot lose my mind because I have the mind of Christ and because I have the mind of Christ, I cannot lose." These were my mantras, my, "Bridge of Awareness" that allowed me to finally cross over into the "Promised Land."

I learned that by quieting myself and meditating on truth I could develop an even greater awareness. I set aside time each day for this practice. At first it was very short, five or ten minutes. I would sit down comfortably, with my feet on the floor, my eyes closed. I would take some slow, deep breaths through my nose. Cool air in, warm moist air out. Slowly, I would open the top of my head and let God's Light and Love pour into my body. It is warm and golden like honey. It flows down the right side of my body, through my mind, over my eyes, jaw, mouth, neck, shoulder, breast, belly, hip, leg and foot. As it makes its way through my body, all the toxins of fear, intolerance, shame and hopelessness stick to it. It goes out my right foot into Mother Earth to be cleansed and healed. I become aware of a warm sensation in my left foot as she sends back the Love and Light up my body in the form of a warm, green light. The light travels up the leg, hip, belly, breast, shoulder, neck, mouth, jaw, eye and mind. This is what I call a "Truth Transfusion."

In this peaceful place, I visualize myself as a beautiful lotus blossom floating down a calm river. I am basking in God's loving sunshine. Oh, it feels so good! I can hear the bubbling of the water. I can smell how sweet and lovely I am. Floating, floating on the "Water of Faith." As I come back to my body, I slowly open my eyes and in gratitude I say "thank you." I am now in touch with my true self and can go through my day being Light, and being of service or mentoring others. This is the face of God – to see Divine light in others. This is true freedom.

CHAPTER 38

*"I am the Lord your God, who brought you out of
the land of Egypt, out of the house of bondage.
You shall have no other gods before me"*

Exodus 20:2,3

First we must relearn that God is not
separate from ourselves and the Bible is really a
story of our spiritual evolution. Spiritually, the
name Moses means "drawing out"[2] and the
name Egypt means "the darkness of ignorance"[3].
The Exodus therefore represents for us a coming
out of the darkness of consciousness limited to
material senses and awakening to divine truth
through spiritual infusion.

<u>My Exodus</u>
Due to the fact that I even "chose" to leave
Egypt tells me that God is pleased with me.
Therefore I am pleased with myself because, at
that time, I thought Egypt was a great ride for
me.

---

2 www.unitydelawareohio.org/moses
3 www.unitydelawareohio.org/moses

I wonder if there are others – party girls or prostitutes – that left their Egypt and "found themselves", like me. You can be a prostitute to anything, you know. It doesn't matter if you are male or female. Anytime you give your power away to something other than yourself, you are prostituting yourself and your soul. Think about that one!

After I left my personal "Egypt", I spent a long time in the Valley of Disenchantment and Disillusionment. However, I just kept going. I went to church and Bible studies; I did outreach and was married while journeying through these valleys. I believe that if you "stand in your truth", it will propel you to the next spiritual level, no matter what it looks like to the external world. I wanted a turning point in my life. My wish was honored.

Proof of my having reached a turning point lies in the fact that I showed some old friends this new path in life. For the last 23 years, I had stayed in touch with old friends from San Diego. I was a "light" to them, a "Wayshower" -- I survived the ugly years. The proof? The wife of the biggest drug lord in Southern California for three decades is now a Born-Again Christian doing street outreach in Vegas. Imagine how powerful her stories are!

I have surrendered all for the sake of seeking and finding the Truth. I live with a deep trust in wisdom, goodness and faith. I am the dancer and the dance, the seeker and the sought-after, the knower and the known. I HAVE COME HOME TO MYSELF.

This is not an ending, but a beginning – the dance goes on.

Let's go on this great journey together and we will be guided by a "Cloud of Truth" and "Pillar of Passion" as the Israelites were - every step of the way. Exodus 14:13 says: "Do not be afraid. Stand firm and you will see the deliverance the Lord will bring you today. The Egyptians you see today you will never see again."

CHAPTER 39

Leaving Egypt

As I said previously, Egypt spiritually means "the darkness of ignorance," but physically speaking, Egypt represents a place of wealth and prosperity. During the great famine of that time, the Israelites sojourned to Egypt because they knew that grain and other needed provisions were abundantly available.

Egypt was a grand place with something to please every desire. There were beautiful palaces and temples with golden idols. The markets were filled to overflowing with food and goods of all kinds. Women of the night with their perfumed oils satisfied even the most sordid desires. Life seemed perfect.

As time passed, the rulers of the Kingdom were no longer peaceful; they became greedy. They wanted to build a city that would be greater than anything that had existed before. In order to accomplish this they needed manpower. Ah, yes, the Israelites! They were not citizens. These people were healthy and there were millions of them. A decree was issued and the Israelites were rounded up and ordered to begin making bricks, hauling rocks, digging ditches and stomping straw. Four Hundred years passed. The great city of Egypt and the pyramids were built. The Israelites found themselves a society of broken, confused slaves living in poverty under Egypt's rule.

It came to pass that the Spirit of God spoke to Moses and told him that he had been chosen to lead his people out of bondage. Even though he had been raised in an Egyptian palace, Moses knew in his spirit that he really was an Israelite. After battling with doubt he accepted the assignment. Moses led approximately six million people out of Egypt and across the desert to "The Promised Land".

So, have you ever been to a spiritual Egypt? Was there something that drew you there for its grandeur? Was there something there that you needed or wanted? Did you, perhaps, follow a friend there? Perhaps you are in this glittering land in the middle of a mess right now and that is why you are reading this book. You *can* have your "Spiritual Awakening", your "Spiritual Exodus".

How can you tell if you are in this spiritual Egypt?

- If you have given your power to anything or anyone.
- If your dreams and goals have been stolen.
- If your identity has been stolen (spiritually speaking)
- If you have more suffering than peace and joy.
- If you are allowing a parasite to suck the life out of you for its personal gain.

Let us return to the Israelites and see how they are doing on their trip to the Promised Land.

The people were moaning and groaning "Where are we going? What are we going to eat?" There was doubt, doubt and more doubt. Moses became completely overwhelmed trying to help all these people by himself so, following the advice of his brother, Aaron, he assigned tribes, and leaders or priests to each tribe. Therefore, the people could rule and care for one another rather than being led by one ruler, as had been the case in Egypt. Most importantly, Moses went to The Source for guidance. He spent time on the mountain, with God, and when he came down, the Shekinah Glory shown so brightly on him that the people could not look upon him.

Have you ever spent time with God and felt like you were glowing?

Moses was constantly tested on the "Trip" and with each miracle, his faith grew stronger. Has your faith grown stronger as you realize God's hand has been providing for you or have you built idols to worship? What an example for the people Moses was! Here they are, still looking for provision after 40 years! They had water and fresh manna to eat everyday. Their shoes did not wear out in 40 years of wandering. They were guided by a cloud during the day and a pillar of fire by night. When it stopped, they stopped. Even with all these miracles, they still didn't "get" it. It took them 40 years to make an eleven day trip! Because of their murmuring, complaining and doubt, they, figuratively, had to go around the mountain one more time.

How long is it going to take before you cross the desert of life into God's land of promises and blessings? It was not until the original generation that left Egypt had died that the Israelites were allowed to enter the Promised Land. Even Moses, because of his anger and frustration with his people, was not allowed to enter into the Promised Land. Before he died, however, because of his faith, God allowed him to see it.

CHAPTER 40

In The Promised Land

The Promised Land is finding out who you really are. You need to "bring back", that is, you need to remember that inner, sacred domain which is the source and goal of the soul. The inner domain or Promised Land contains the unity of life and consciousness which, though you once possessed it, has been lost. Now you must find it again. When our physical journey aligns with our energy bodies this experience is even more powerful.

On my physical journey I brought this self-confidence into the next "season" of my life – as a very successful hair dresser. But even the Promised Land has its Giants that you encounter and one of the most insidious is identity theft. I allowed my identity to be stolen once again by all the drugs that I did and by allowing my life to be a façade of happiness. Giving my identity away again took all my time, energy and money.... my son and I wound up homeless!

The next time I gave away my identity I was a Department head at the Defense Department in Boston. I was no more created to work in an office than an eagle is to be kept in a cage. But I was successful! Oh, yes! I had the confidence, the clothes and the charisma. My department ran like a fine-tuned instrument. I received numerous awards. My son and I had a home in the country. I had a camper. I was making it happen again. The truth is that in order to maintain all of this I took enough valium every day for five years to tranquilize a small elephant; I coupled that with cocaine and wine cocktails. It was all about the money!

By the end of this "season" I was "fried". You see, when we allow identity theft to happen in our lives, it steals everything from us. However if we stand in the Truth of who we really are, we are restored. It was at this point that I became a born-again Christian. I figured I could trust Jesus so I thought I would run with Him for awhile.

As always, I jumped in with both feet. This time was it was different. Because of the 20 years of drug use and the lifestyle that went with it, I couldn't get a hold of myself. As a follower of the Christ I was in "the wilderness of my mind". Oh, I was still serving. I was teaching Bible scriptures to preteen girls at my church, running a bus ministry, outfitting inner city kids for camp, etc. But through all of these years and successes, I HAD NO IDEA WHO I WAS. To all intense and purposes, I was a sinner saved by grace. I was the head and not the tail, I was blessed going in and blessed going out. I was on the good path. I was a good friend. I tried to be a good wife and mother. I kept a clean house and cooked from scratch. I tried to be the "Proverbs Woman", just like my friends.

This was just what I did. Because I had lost myself, I couldn't love myself. Because I couldn't love myself, I couldn't love anyone else. Yes, I was affectionate but that is as far as it went. I was still on the merry-go-round.

I'm sharing this with you so that you can see what identity theft looks like. First, through all of the confusion you begin to realize that you don't know who you are. Secondly, you learn that your identity is not what you do but really it is your soul, your mind, your will, your emotions; it is your divine creation.

There are other Giants to deal with. I call one group Psychic Vampires. They steal your soul and they will continue to do so in various ways until they kill you, if you let them. You are still on the merry-go-round. So how can you get off? By listening to your belly, praying, meditating, letting your awareness of the truth of who you really are bubble up from inside of you. Then, when you are ready, go find yourself a mentor. He or she will teach you truths that will allow your divine soul, your divine creation, your true self to blossom.

CHAPTER 41

Again, as I go through my day in the "Promised Land," I realize there are still other Giants to conquer. I call one group of giants "Predators". They are disguised as people who love you. They are pros at being interested in the same things you are at first meeting. Then they have a need. Be watchful.

How do I conquer and kill any invader in the promised land of my spirit? I do it by using my awareness. Is that energy positive or negative? How has that invader handled past relationships? Again, I listen to my belly. Just as David killed the giant Goliath with a rock, so can I. I pull back my "Sling of Awareness" and hit the "giants" with a "Rock of Truth". Standing firmly in my own truth I watch as they go down because they cannot survive in Truth. I remember who I am; I take back my identity and continue on my journey.

Sometimes I come upon "Giants of Impatience". In my excitement of wanting more awareness, more wisdom I sometimes get ahead of Spirit. Have you ever heard the saying "I was so upset I was beside myself?" This is because you are not aligned with your true self. I have had to train myself, to quickly become aware of how I am feeeeling. "A Course in Miracles"[4] states, "Those who are certain of the outcome

---

[4] A Course in Miracles, Teaching Manual, Page 15

can afford to wait, and without anxiety." This is why patience is a spiritual virtue.

I must focus on how my desired outcome will feel -- blessed, joyful, content. My affirmation for this is, "I've got all the time I need and I am certain of the outcome. I will allow it to show up as it will in due time." This allows me to kill the "Giants of Impatience" and continue on my journey in peace.

On occasion I feel that my journey is slowing down. This almost always means that I have been confronted with a, "Giant of Self-Sabotage." Through stillness and meditation I become aware that I am not steadily moving in the right direction. As I go deeper inside I become aware of old underlying patterns; I must free myself from them. Centering myself, I find the wisdom inside the wound. When I honor it I allow it to change me and kill the giant.

So if I was created in love and awareness, where did it go? Over my lifetime I have been conditioned and addicted to others' belief systems because I had no self-love. I just kept hopping on merry-go-rounds of false relationships, finances, hopelessness and addictions of all sorts. Yes, I did great works with sincerity and passion but when I went home I would still overeat, argue and cry. I was still wearing my "Spiritual Shackles." I continually felt like I had a ball and chain on my leg holding me back. I was denying awareness of my true divine nature. As I continue on this journey of self-love I am aware of a great transformation taking place in my spirit. I feel lighter and stronger as I bask in God's love. I am willing to love myself. My confidence is blossoming; I have a lotus center of self-love. It plants its roots deep down in the darkest, muddiest, murkiest places, grows toward the light, and then – inevitably basks in the sunshine. While developing, this most beautiful blossom withstands floods, droughts and all kinds of storms in its environment. When it is ready, this sacred flower opens and unfolds. Each fragrant petal represents an awareness of happiness, connection, patience, faith, long-suffering, and wisdom; each one is attached to a bud of self-love.

If I stand in my truth and remember who I am I will be free to heal. Free to love myself. Free to love others. Free to be a warrior. Free to love God. Free to serve others. Free to mentor others. Free to have my miracles. I am not in bondage any longer and little Nanci is happy. For this I am forever grateful.

EPILOGUE

I thought I had seen and done it all. I thought I had made it through. I believed my lotus was blooming. I had hope and peace and love. Then it happened. I was diagnosed with cancer.

My boat of cancer arrived in my life on January 23, 2012, in the form of lumps in the lymph nodes of my neck. I was hospitalized for a DVT in my right leg (blood clot). The previous August I had been diagnosed with Factor V Leiden clotting disorder while in the hospital for an infected blood clot in my left jugular vein. When my oncologist came in to check my leg, I asked him what the lumps were on the side of my neck and in my armpit. He ordered a biopsy of a lemon-sized lump under my left armpit and sent me home. For two weeks I waited and prayed that it wouldn't be cancer. My son went with me to the doctor's office for the diagnosis. It was cancer. A squamous cell renegade type had settled in the lymph nodes and was in nine areas of my body. He said I had a 25 percent chance of even managing it. He also said there would be four to six chemo treatments which would include one week inpatient hospitalization every 21 days (because of the clotting disorder). The first one would be right away.

During this time, a message came to me saying that my spirit is fine. It does not have any illness. It is just my earth-suit that needs to be fixed. Wow! That gave me a whole new perspective on the situation. I was able to realize that cancer cannot affect my Spirit. It was all about what I *thought* that affected the cancer. I shared this with my oncologist and he said, "That's profound."

To my way of thinking, cancer is a boat. A vessel that will take you some place you have never been and give you something you have never had. You cannot play with cancer on any terms but its own. But I will tell you that the cancer became secondary during my first week of chemo. I spent my time ministering to others; that became my priority. Nurses came in regularly to talk and the doctor, during his night rounds, would stop, sit and visit with me. He said, "Even though it is the midnight hour, you never cease to inspire me". That is when I became aware that something was happening. I was becoming a vessel of light and love. Illness cannot live in a pure, clean vessel and that is when I knew that I had to take inventory of all my feelings and thoughts.

I thought about forgiveness, of myself and of others. I had to put the ugly thoughts in a boat and send them on their way. Anger, bitterness, resentment, hate and fear – they all had to go into that boat and they had to go on their way. I wanted to be a clean vessel spiritually, physically and emotionally so I could heal.

For the next three months I worked on this continuously. Every morning I visualized two boats pulling up to my shore. One was dark, slimy and rotting and the other one was glittery gold and white and clean. I could choose one for the day. If I took the dark slimy one it would take me down a dark jungle-like river. I would be lost, confused, exhausted and sad. How could I succeed like this?

If I took the glittery gold one, it would take me to a bright blue ocean of vast possibilities. The sun was bright and warm on my shoulders; the sparkling sea-shine showed me beautiful visions of things to come and joy soared in my heart. I could win if I stayed in this boat!

Months of treatments passed. I allowed myself to be broken and cleansed by the glitter boat of cancer. My son and I went back to the oncologist and he said the cancer was gone and that I had surely experienced "Divine intervention". He acknowledged that because my original diagnosis was so incredibly severe. It was difficult to wrap my brain around a miracle of this magnitude! He wanted me to have one more week of chemo to be sure there were no residual cells lying around.

In my mind, cancer took me to a beautiful place where I could let go, forgive and forget. It gave me the greatest gift of all – my Higher Self. This "Higher Self" is where the visions and the messages come from.

Undoubtedly this latest challenge was, at the very least unexpected, but I was led to board that glittery boat and able then to head into the "Promised Land". All the while, little Nanci, continued to sing, "Row, row, row your boat, gently down the stream..." May your journey be filled with light, truth, love, gratitude and songs.

Here I stand and remain forever yours -- a Grateful Lotus.

ABOUT THE AUTHOR

Nanci Reason is an author and motivational speaker on subjects such as a lifetime of drugs and surviving cancer. She has worked in construction, the beauty industry and the U.S. Defense Department. She will lift you up with her winning combination of humor and practical spirituality and help you find your inner self. She currently lives in Mesa, Arizona.

To learn more go to:
www.unlimitedmiracleproductions.com

www.ingramcontent.com/pod-product-compliance
Lightning Source LLC
Chambersburg PA
CBHW072126090426
42739CB00012B/3081